An Introduction to
Roman Religion

This book is dedicated to those who first saw it taking shape.

An Introduction to Roman Religion

John Scheid
Translated by Janet Lloyd

INDIANA
University Press
Bloomington & Indianapolis

This book is a publication of

Indiana University Press
601 North Morton Street
Bloomington, Indiana 47404-3797 USA

http://iupress.indiana.edu

Telephone orders	800-842-6796
Fax orders	812-855-7931
Orders by e-mail	iuporder@indiana.edu

Translation © Janet Lloyd, 2003

First published in North America in 2003 by Indiana University Press

First published in English in 2003 by Edinburgh University Press Ltd

First published in France as *La religion des Romans*
© Armand Colin/Masson, Paris, 1998

The right of John Scheid
to be identified as author of this work
has been asserted in accordance with
the Copyright, Designs and Patents Act 1988.

Typeset in Bembo and Century Gothic
by Bibliocraft Ltd, Dundee, and
printed and bound in Great Britain by
MPG Books Ltd, Bodmin

Library of Congress Cataloging-in-Publication Data

Scheid, John.
  [Religion des Romans. English]
  An introduction to Roman religion / John Scheid ; translated
by Janet Lloyd.
    p. cm.
Includes bibliographical references and index.
  ISBN 0-253-34377-1 (alk. paper) – ISBN 0-253-21660-5
(pbk. : alk. paper)
  1. Rome–Religion. I. Lloyd, Janet. II. Title.
  BL803.S3413 2003
  292.07–dc21

                         2003007470

1 2 3 4 5 08 07 06 05 04 03

CONTENTS

LIST OF TEXT BOXES

PUBLISHER'S ACKNOWLEDGEMENT

The publisher wishes to thank Lady Lloyd for translating the book, Dr Mary Beard for her work in preparing the book for English-speaking readers, the author for his help during both processes, and the French Ministry of Culture for the award of a subvention towards the cost of translation.

Introduction

Roman religion does not speak for itself, although we might imagine that it did. Rome is no more, and its culture and religion long dead, but we still use the same religious vocabulary. 'Religion', 'piety', 'deity', 'sacrifice', 'ritual', superstition', 'temple' and 'altar' are all words that have survived down the centuries. That continuity alone seems to guarantee that no misunderstanding is possible.

Yet this apparent closeness to us masks many differences. Western culture may still today be the legacy of Rome, but that does not mean that the Romans were just like ourselves. On many points, in particular religion, the Romans were very different from us. Besides, even the term 'the Romans' covers a multitude of people, identities and cultures. What, after all, was a Roman? A citizen of Rome itself or of Latium? And in what period? At the time of the Punic Wars, at the beginning of the common era, or under the Empire? The cultural identity of a 'Roman' differed from one period to another. From the first century BC onward, he might have been a native of a city in Italy – a city in Umbria, Etruria or Magna Graecia – and soon even of a city overseas. Under the Empire, there were 'Romans' throughout the Roman world; some were descended from emigrants from Rome and Italy, others were naturalised foreigners (*peregrini*). Did they all share the same culture? Nor should we forget that Roman citizens represented a definite minority of the inhabitants of the Roman world. Up until the first century BC even most of the free inhabitants of Italy were excluded from full citizenship, and only in AD 212 did all free *peregrini* become Roman citizens. And, of course, all these extensions of citizenship did not affect the very large numbers of slaves, but applied to the free population only.

All this means that it is almost impossible to speak of 'Roman religion' in any general, inclusive sense. A choice has to be made.

This book will take 'Romans' to mean all Roman citizens and their dependants living in Rome or some other Roman city. When it comes to naturalised Romans, I shall consider only their 'Roman' religious behaviour. I shall not try to reconstruct their original native religion or (even if I could) to evaluate how those two religious attitudes may have interacted. The most easily identifiable 'Roman' modes of religious behaviour are the rituals of public cult; so it is here at the institutional level, the first to be affected by such influences and transformations, that we can at least raise the problems of acculturation. As the situation becomes extremely complex from the beginning of the common era on, I shall primarily be focusing on the city of Rome and also on Roman colonies and *municipia*, leaving the reader to adapt the major principles to local circumstances, if need be.

Given the differences between the religion of the Romans and those of the modern Western world, some discussion of theory and method must precede the main part of the book; so three preliminary chapters will set out the major problems facing anyone wishing to study Roman religion, and explain the principles and ideas upon which it was founded. Later chapters will concentrate on rituals, cult, sacred space and divination. Various different strands will then come together in the examination of the status of priesthood and divinity in Roman religion; and further details will be given about specialised religious communities. The last part will consider the problem of 'exegesis' in Roman religion.

The book is conceived from a thematic rather than a chronological standpoint, unlike most recent textbooks currently available. But for easy reference, the chronology includes a list of important religious events.

Part I
Questions of Methodology

Chapter 1
Problems and problematics

There is no innocent way to approach a religious system, even when that religion has been dead for fifteen centuries. Consciously or not, historians tend to project their own beliefs onto the religion they are studying. As a result, they may misconstrue the facts to the point of negating them.

1 MODERN INFLUENCES ON THE STUDY OF ROMAN RELIGION

Modern studies of Roman religion have not avoided that particular problem. Since the mid-nineteenth century, when it first became the subject of specialist research, the study of Roman religion has been affected by a variety of influences. Christianity, in particular, has often provided the yardstick by which it has been judged. The fact that it was under the Roman Empire that Christianity developed seemed to justify the generally disparaging judgement passed on traditional Roman ritualistic polytheism. It seemed to support the notion that a 'superior', 'true' religion had triumphed over an 'inferior' one, and to justify writing of the 'conversion' of the Romans.

1.1 A decadent religion?

Historians for a long time characterised traditional Roman religion as cold and decadent. This approach was very much due to the sway of German idealism, which was such a powerful inspiration for classical studies throughout the nineteenth century, and in particular to the example set by the famous German historian Theodor Mommsen. On this view Roman religion had been moribund and treated with cynicism by the Romans themselves for most of its history; and yet, it was argued, this religion would originally have been founded upon an extremely strong popular piety that was ready to show itself again, irresistibly, as soon as a 'true' religion appeared on the scene. This approach never managed to produce a clear explanation for this endless and improbable religious decadence that would have lasted for close on ten centuries, nor did it explain what was meant by 'popular piety'. The fact was that the scholars who advocated it regarded the development of religion through the lens of Christianity: some, like Mommsen himself, using the history of Roman religion to ridicule priests and superstitions, and to counter the influence of the Catholic Church in Germany, others seeing it as a stage in the progressive ascent to Christianity.

1.2 A religion swamped by 'foreign cults'?

A second, related, tendency set great store by the contrast between original cults, on the one hand, those that were supposedly 'typically' Roman, and newer 'foreign' ones, on the other. This idea stemmed from a perfectly justified project of Josef A. Hartung's, in a book entitled *Die Religion der Römer nach den Quellen dargestellt* (*The Religion of the Romans, Described According to the Ancient Sources*) and published in 1836, to separate the religion of the Romans from that of the Greeks. At the beginning of the nineteenth century, it was still common to treat the two religions as essentially one and the same thing, to refer to 'Greek myths' when discussing Roman religion, and to call the Greek goddess Athena by her Roman title 'Minerva'.

Some perspectives that, for many years, determined the modern view of Roman religion

While abstraction, which lies at the foundation of every religion, elsewhere endeavoured to rise to wider and more enlarged conceptions and to penetrate ever more deeply into the essence of things, the forms of the ▶

▶ Roman faith remained at, or sank to, a singularly low level of conception and insight . . . [The religion of Rome] was unable to excite the mysterious awe after which the human heart has always a longing, or thoroughly to embody the incomprehensible and even the malignant elements in nature and in man, which must not be wanting in religion if it would reflect man as a whole.

The Latin religion sank into an incredible insipidity and dullness, and early became shrivelled into an anxious and dreary round of ceremonies.

Theodor Mommsen, *The History of Rome (1854)*, trans. William Purdie Dickson, London, (vol. 1, pp. 212, 222) 1996

Perhaps there never was a religion so cold and so prosaic as the Roman. Being subordinated to politics, it sought, above all, to secure the protection of the gods for the state and to avert the effects of their malevolence by the strict execution of proper practices. It entered into a contract with the celestial powers from which mutual obligations arose: sacrifices on one side, favors on the other. The pontiffs, who were also magistrates, regulated the religious practices with the exact precision of jurists; as far as we know, the prayers were all couched in formulas as dry and verbose as notarial instruments. The liturgy reminds one of the ancient civil law on account of the minuteness of its prescriptions. This religion looked suspiciously at the abandonment of the soul to the ecstasies of devotion. It repressed, by force if necessary, the exuberant manifestations of too ardent faith and everything that was not in keeping with the grave dignity befitting the relations of a *civis Romanus* with a god. The Jews had the same scrupulous respect as the Romans for a religious code and formulas of the past, 'but' [in the words of Salomon Reinach], 'in spite of their dry and minute practices, the legalism of the Pharisees stirred the heart more strongly than did Roman formalism'.

Franz Cumont, *The Oriental Religions in Roman Paganism (1806)*, trans. Grant Showerman, Chicago, 1911 (pp. 28–9)

However, this necessary separation of Greek from Roman was likewise influenced by the Romantic concept of closed, 'pure' cultures and by the idea of decadence – as if true Roman religion only existed before its contamination by decadent imports from the outside. And that influence can also be seen in the greatest ever handbook on Roman religion, *Religion und Kultus der Römer* (*Roman Religion and*

Cult) by Georg Wissowa (2nd edn, 1912). In this, Wissowa tried to distinguish between two, opposed, categories of gods: those who were *indigetes* or 'original' (in a misleadingly loose sense of the term) and the *novensides*, those who were newly installed. This distinction was pushed to such absurd extremes that even the triad of Capitoline deities (Jupiter, Juno and Minerva), the guardian gods of the Roman state, were represented as being of foreign origin. Be that as it may, according to this view, the transformation of Roman religion would already have begun in the archaic period. In this context, the incorporation into Rome of certain deities who originated in Greek areas of Asia Minor is always considered a fact of central importance and at the same time a 'non-Roman' feature. Such cults, known in general as 'oriental', are condemned as having distorted the 'old' Roman religion and are consequently treated as if they formed a quite separate religious category, which heralded either the decadence of the Romans (as in the case of the cult of Cybele), or the advent of Christianity (in the case of Egyptian Isis, or Persian Mithras).

1.3 The myth of a 'pure' religion

The third thesis that exerted a profound influence on historians of religion is the 'myth of origins'. According to this, the 'purity' of a religion mattered more than its history and (or so the argument went) it was only at its origins, that is to say outside history, that a tradition could be defined as 'pure'. Many handbooks on Roman religion devoted numerous pages to its origins and the influences that it subsequently underwent; in some cases entire books were based on theories about these originary phases of Roman religion. The origins that were most favoured and received most emphasis were Indo-European and Etruscan. However, as we shall see, that idea that one might be able to reconstruct a 'pure', unadulterated state of Roman religion is itself a modern myth.

2 HOW MUCH DO WE KNOW ABOUT ARCHAIC ROMAN RELIGION?

2.1 A limited number of sources

The reconstruction of the origins, or at least of the earliest imaginable period, of Roman religion poses a number of problems. The first relates to evidence. All the sources of any length that explicitly concern religion date from the late Republic and the Empire. It is extremely difficult to go back any further than the second century BC. All that we have from the archaic period, in the strict sense of the term, is a handful of difficult epigraphical texts and, above all, archaeological data. It is hardly surprising then that many historians follow the account – anachronistic as it is – which the Romans themselves gave of those early days. The consequence is that these historians retroject into the remote past facts and attitudes that clearly date from much later, and are apt to attribute an archaic character to all 'typically' Roman behaviour.

So we may be suspicious of both the title and the aims of the large volume in which Georges Dumézil, perhaps the most distinguished and influential twentieth-century French scholar of Roman religion, summarised his theories and principal lines of research. His famous book, entitled *Archaic Roman Religion*, in fact deals almost exclusively with documents and evidence dating not to the archaic period at all but to the last two centuries of the Republic. Dumézil's plan was to reconstruct the Roman religion of archaic times but, despite his brilliant analyses (to which we shall return), the religious attitudes reconstructed seem to relate more to the contemporaries of Cato and Augustus than to those of Romulus. But it is only fair to note that, from Dumézil's own point of view, this would not necessarily have made any difference. For, as an Indo-Europeanist rather than a student of Roman religion alone, Dumézil was ultimately more interested in the timeless structures common to all societies which share Indo-European languages than in the precise historical period during which these structures first made their appearance. In the case of Rome, his principal concern was to show how closely the earliest religious structures he could detect matched those of other Indo-European societies. So, for example, he investigated the meaning of the fire of the goddess Vesta in relation to sacrificial fires in other Indo-European cultures, drawing particularly on models described in Vedic texts.

2.2 The difficulties of using them

Before attempting to exploit such evidence as we do possess for the earliest phases of Roman religion, we need to assess it carefully. Some of it will turn out to be authentic vestiges of the distant past. Some will remain ambiguous and will therefore be difficult to use to reconstruct the religious attitudes and practices of the archaic period. Recent studies have reached the conclusion that when Roman antiquarians themselves reconstructed the archaic history of Rome and Latium, they based their arguments not on reliable knowledge that had been handed down, but on deductions and guesswork from place names, religious functions, rituals and a few written documents: in short, on vestiges of the past that were more or less ancient and more or less ambiguous. But what should we make of the stories woven from this by the contemporaries of Timaeus, of Cato or of Livy? The considerable and spectacular archaeological material that excavations have brought to light over the past half-century provide far more reliable evidence, even though this hardly ever resolves the question of the authenticity of the literary tradition.

Needless to say, if it is to be credible, our use of the sources must match the standards of modern scholarship. Roman myths must be analysed in the historical context of their production; their meanings must be interpreted according to the methods of structural myth-analysis. Evidence from language and linguistic structures cannot be fathomed by mere intuitive guesses, but must be elucidated according to the strict rules of comparative linguistics. Cultural comparativism must take into account the ongoing evolution of this discipline and can no longer be satisfied by superficial comparisons borrowed from the anthropology of the 1900s.

Despite all the historical problems that they pose, Dumézil's careful analyses of Roman myths, language and institutions provide an incomparable methodological model for the use and interpretation of sources. To return to sacrificial fires, for example, Dumézil based his theory on a detailed analysis of all aspects of the ritual: the circular or rectangular shape of the altars concerned, the layout of the Forum and the relationship between the fire of Vesta and the (destructive) fire of Vulcan. And one of his central topics was the so-called 'tri-functional' ideology that has often been seen as characteristic of Indo-European religion in general (where the role of the sovereign, the warrior and the producer are the main structuring principles of both society and religion). So, for example, Dumézil analysed a little-known (and barely studied) inscribed text recording one particular expiatory ritual carried out by the priesthood of the Arval Brethren. Here he not only highlighted the different functions of the different deities involved in the ritual, he also showed that even under the Empire the priests still seem to have been conscious of the structures of this underlying Indo-European tripartite division. In short, what distinguishes his method of work is a minute and exhaustive analysis of every aspect of the evidence, a method strongly influenced by that of the earlier French anthropologists Marcel Mauss and Marcel Granet.

3 THE PROBLEM OF ORIGINS

Among the major influences on archaic Roman religion, scholars have appealed to a primitive (or 'predeistic') strand of thought, to the Etruscans and to the Indo-Europeans.

3.1 The primitivists

Ludwig Deubner's primitivist or 'predeist' theories were for many years extremely influential in Roman studies, for they

seemed to correspond to the unsophisticated and conserva-
tive image of Roman piety. The idea was that the most archaic
Roman rituals (though how one is supposed to recognise 'the
most archaic rituals' is far from clear) were embedded in an
extremely ancient period of religious history, a period prior to
the development of the idea of deity (that is, '*pre*deist'). In the
time before gods, there were only religious *actions*.

This type of research was based on the wide-ranging,
catch-all theories of nineteenth-century religious anthropology, with its fertility cults, cults of mother-goddesses, natural
elements and the stars. Above all, it assumed that archaic
religions were necessarily ritualistic. A stress on ritual was
seen, in other words, as a key distinguishing mark of archaic
religion in general. Primitivist theories were very influential
up until the 1960s, and in Britain were particularly associated
with the work of H. J. Rose. But even as early as the 1920s
they were opposed by the followers of Walter F. Otto (the
group known as the Frankfurt School), and, as theories, they
are now abandoned. However, the logical short cuts and the
rather too easy explanations that they allowed themselves
continue to exert an influence in the field.

3.2 The Etruscans

Other hypotheses on the origin of the Roman religion are
more serious and more problematic. The Etruscans, Rome's
neighbours in Italy, with a history stretching back to a time
before Rome's foundation, are frequently imagined as the
origin of this or that Roman institution. Roman divination, in
particular, is claimed to stem largely from Etruscan practices
and theories – as the ancients themselves said it did. But in
the total absence of any means of verifying their claims and
because much of the religion of the Etruscan cities is still
impenetrable to us, such references explain nothing. So, at
the moment, it is not possible to provide any satisfactory
answer to the question of how influential the Etruscans were
on the origins of Roman religion.

3.3 The Indo-Europeans

The Indo-European hypothesis – that cultures which share Indo-European languages ultimately derive their religious and other institutions from some primitive Indo-European society, now lost in the mists of time – poses different problems. Quite apart from the difficulties mentioned above (such as, what counts as archaic?), which affect all quests for origins, reference to the Indo-Europeans raises an extra question. The idea of some original, primitive Indo-European society is based on similarities in language, myth and ritual structure in various cultures distant both in date and in place, from India to Ireland. But even if such similarities are not illusory (and in some cases, they are almost certainly not), this resolves nothing. For what do the resemblances signify? And how should the far more numerous differences be interpreted? Above all, what can an 'Indo-European' feature or set of features in a culture possibly explain? Where do they come from? How did they develop? Does the real meaning of such a feature in Rome stem from that mythical past, did it exist in the same form in that 'Indo-European' past, or was it formed in the historical society in which this feature is attested? Quite apart from the general problem posed by the actual historicity of the original primitive Indo-European society that this theory postulates, clearly every element in a culture has developed in a precise historical and social context. That is primarily what constitutes a cultural heritage; and to establish it is a difficult enough task even for historical times. To try to get back beyond history may be an exciting undertaking but it is of an altogether different order.

4 WHAT RELIGION FOR ARCHAIC ROME?

4.1 Putting origins to good use

Research into the influences on the early culture and religion of the Romans is not in itself an absurd project. But such a study cannot be expected to explain everything. The quest for origins is interesting, for it illuminates the pluralistic and mixed nature of all cultures, or should aim to do so. The criticisms expressed above apply not so much to the principle of the research itself as to how it is carried out. They are aimed, in the first place, at the historicist mania for breaking down all institutions into elements said to have 'come from' somewhere else, without taking into account the fact that cultural borrowing is always generated by an internal need and that it always transforms whatever is taken from the other culture. As for the influences so often invoked, we may well wonder why they are assumed to work in the 'right' way only during the archaic period, but to be a sign of decadence later. When is a culture reckoned to be 'itself'? Why eliminate from the defining elements of a culture all influences later than the archaic period? For example, in the case of Rome, why eliminate Hellenism? And why, even in the archaic period, are the Greek and Phoenician influences from the eastern Mediterranean generally excluded? If one accepts that Roman culture was subject to outside influences, it is necessary to take into account all the 'borrowings' that took place in the course of its history. To seek to limit influence to one single culture (that of the Etruscans or Indo-Europeans, for example) boils down to laying claim to some kind of exclusively Roman 'purity' or identity. Attempts have already been made to draw attention to a Greek or Cypriot influence on archaic Roman religion. But these efforts, laudable as they are, will only work successfully if they obey the strict rules of cultural comparativism (such as those adopted by modern social anthropology, or in the careful comparative analyses of Dumézil).

4.2 A critical perspective on studies of archaic Rome
We are still a long way from being able to summarise any agreed position on archaic Roman religion. Even the earliest research in the subject, by Franz Altheim, for example, or Dumézil, remains controversial and is still under discussion. The most interesting and persistently useful parts of their work are not so much the grand theories as their analyses of

limited and precise case studies. Dumézil's method was always first to examine the evidence within its own context and only then to compare the Roman data to similar structures in the wider Indo-European world (as more recently Walter Burkert has always looked carefully at the evidence before moving on to his own more elaborate and sometimes strange theories). So even if, as we have seen, Dumézil's comparison of Roman religious structures with those of other Indo-European societies leads principally to further questions, his careful analysis of the surviving evidence often constitutes a real methodological breakthrough – throwing light, for example, on the *modus operandi* of various shadowy deities and explaining, as no one had done before, their significance within Roman religion. By combining the philological methods of Wissowa with a more anthropological *savoir faire*, Dumézil effectively invented the religious anthropology of the Romans. That certainly is the first important outcome of his work – whether or not one is interested in his overarching Indo-European project.

Moreover, intense work on the history of archaic Rome and Italy carried out over the past twenty or so years has prompted first-rate archaeological excavations and a new critique of the written sources. Here too, the primary result of these researches probably lies in the excellent quality of the publications produced and of the debate as a whole, rather than in the conclusions reached. The temple of Castor and Pollux in the Roman Forum is a case in point: recent archaeological exploration has provided clear evidence that it dates back to the fifth century BC; all earlier discussions on the subject had amounted to no more than marginal glosses on Livy's claims that it had been founded in the 490s, after the miraculous appearance of Castor and Pollux at the battle of Lake Regillus.

4.3 A decisive factor: the birth of the city
Until archaeology and the critical analysis of written sources have gradually put together a set of data that is genuinely

'archaic', it seems preferable to concentrate our study of Roman religion on later, better-documented periods. We shall attempt no more than a general overview of the history of the religion in the archaic period and the early years of the Republic.

As with other Roman institutions, the only really important factor in the archaic period is not the arrival of the Indo-Europeans or the presence or expulsion of the Etruscans – hypothetical as those events are. The only decisive change attested in the archaic period is the birth of the city. Archaeology, epigraphy and the recollections transmitted by later sources all show that from the seventh century onward major transformations occurred in Etruria, Latium and Rome – transformations which must be related to the phenomenon of the 'birth of the city'. As in the Greek states, elite groups invented a new system of communal life and government, founded on debate, the acceptance of decisions reached in common, and the guarantee of liberty for all citizens. In Rome this system evolved slowly, eventually becoming, in the fifth century BC, what historians call the Roman Republic. There were all kinds of further changes resulting from the vast growth in Rome's imperial territory, from the civil wars of the first century BC and from the establishment of the form of government known as the Principate, or Empire (from 27 BC onward). But throughout its history Roman institutions were always determined by the model of the city and its ideals. Even when the emperor Augustus and his successors founded a regime many aspects of which were monarchical, they did so, formally at least, within a traditional Republican ideological framework.

In trying to understand the religious behaviour of the ancient Romans, we should never forget the fundamental importance of *city ideology*. As we shall see, that ideal of collective life determined most aspects of religious practice and thought. It is reasonable to suppose that already in the archaic period Roman religion, in its earliest phases, was developing along the path that it continued to follow in the historical period. Or, to put that another way: Roman religion in its historical form established itself in the period that saw the invention of the city.

5 'DECOLONISING' THE RELIGION OF THE ROMANS

Given the problems posed by the sources relating to the archaic period, this book will mainly focus on Roman religion between the third century BC and the third century AD. The centre of attention will not be the various influences that may have affected religious traditions, but the ways that religion functioned and evolved – matters that those obsessed by the origins of religion generally forget to address in a systematic fashion. Readers should already be aware that this book is meant to challenge the premise that Roman religion was decadent, intrinsically cold, and furthermore barbarised by 'Eastern' cults. But none of us can escape our prejudices and the assumptions drawn from our own society and history. Even if we were to bury ourselves in antiquity and read only the ancient sources, we would still hardly be able to guard against those insidious influences. A better tactic is to remain conscious of the weight brought to bear by the recent past and the implicit cultural attitudes which threaten to distort our judgement, and then to act accordingly, with those influences in mind. From this point of view, historical anthropology offers an excellent school of thought and a methodology that will help to distance us from our ethnocentrism and to 'decolonise' (to borrow Jesper Svenbro's expression) the religion of the Romans.

Chapter 2
Definitions, concepts, difficulties

Anyone interested in a religion of the past should beware the pitfall of anachronism. So, right at the start, let us identify a few fundamental features of Roman religion, which are enough to illustrate its 'otherness'. All these features will be studied in greater detail in the course of this book.

1 DEFINITIONS

1.1 Major principles

- This was a religion without revelation, without revealed books, without dogma and without orthodoxy. The central requirement was, instead, what has been called 'orthopraxis', the correct performance of prescribed rituals.

- It was a ritualistic religion and, as such, was strictly traditionalist. But this did not prevent it from evolving and integrating new elements, for openness – to new citizens and to new gods – was itself part of Roman tradition.

- It was a religion in which rituals and ritual attitudes defined and disseminated representations of deities and of the order of things. However cold and self-interested this religion was, it is a mistake to consider it closed to all spiritual ideas and content. Furthermore, religious practice by no means excluded free exegesis and speculation. Nevertheless, such activities took place outside religious life in the strict sense of the term. In so far as the only dogma was the obligation to observe rituals, individuals were perfectly at liberty to conceive of the gods, religion and the world however they pleased.

- It was a religion which kept explicit expression of belief quite separate from religious practice.
- It was a religion that involved no initiation and no teaching. Religious duties were imposed on individuals by their birth, adoption, affranchisement or grant of Roman citizenship (whether as freed slaves or naturalised foreigners). In short, these duties were linked to the social status of an individual and not to any personal decision of a spiritual kind (such as baptism or conversion, for example). Those who did not enjoy the same social status could not belong to the same religious community: in principle, a foreigner had no obligations towards the Roman deities. And if one changed one's status, it was logical also to change one's religion.
- So this was a social religion, closely linked to the community, not to the individual. It involved individuals only in so far as they were members of a particular community. There was in fact no such thing as 'Roman religion', only a series of Roman religions, as many Roman religions as there were Roman social groups: the city, the legion, the various units in the legion, colleges of public servants (*apparitores*), colleges of artisans, sub-districts of the city ('wards' or 'quarters'), families and so on.
- It was a religion with no moral code. The ethical code by which it was ruled was the same as that which ruled other 'non-religious' social relations.
- It was a religion that aimed for the earthly wellbeing of the community, not for the salvation of an individual and his or her immortal soul in the after-life. The gods did help individuals, but primarily in so far as they were members of the community, and only secondarily as

individuals *per se* rather than as people involved in community affairs.

- It follows that there was a religious aspect to every communal action, and a communal aspect to every religious action. Inevitably, therefore, public cult incorporated political aspects. In this sense the Roman religion could be said to be a political religion.
- It was a religion under no particular authority or leader, even at the level of public cult. Religious authority was always shared. Nor did this religion recognise any specific founder, whether divine or sent by God. It was the founders of Rome, of other towns or of individual families who founded the religion of these communities and dictated its rules.
- It was a polytheistic religion. The gods varied according to the community concerned; they were, so to speak, members of the same community as their worshippers.

Definitions of religion
religion . . .

1 *A state of life bound by monastic vows* . . . 3 Action or conduct indicating a *belief in*, reverence for, and desire to please, *a* divine ruling power; the exercise or practice of rites or observances implying this . . . 4 A particular system of *faith* and worship 5 Recognition on the part of man of some higher unseen power *having control of his destiny*, and as being entitled to *obedience*, reverence, and worship; the general mental and *moral* attitude resulting from this *belief*. . . personal or general acceptance of *this feeling* as a standard of *spiritual* and practical life.
Shorter Oxford English Dictionary (3rd edn)

(Those elements at variance with Roman ideas of religion are in italics.)

religion 1 A supernatural feeling of constraint, usu. having the force of prohibition or impediment **b** (pred.) that which is prohibited, taboo; also, a positive obligation, rule. **2** An impediment to action proceeding from doubt, religious awe, conscience, etc., a scruple; (w. gen.) a scruple (with regard to). **3** A state of impediment, etc., consequent on the violation or non-observance of supernatural laws **b** a question involving such an ▶

▶ impediment, etc. **4** A manifestation of divine sanction. **5** A consideration enforcing conformity to a religious or moral principle, a sanction. **6** A sense of the presence of supernatural power, religious fear, awe **b** religious feeling; (w. pejorative force) superstition. **7** A quality (attached to a person, place, object, action, etc.) evoking awe or reverence, sanctity b. (as a quality of gods). **8** The performance of rites, ceremonies, etc., relating to the supernatural, religious observance **b** a religious practice, custom, ritual, or sim. **9** A particular system of religious observance, cult. **10** Punctilious regard for one's obligations, conscientiousness **b** (w.gen.) scrupulous regard (for).

Oxford Latin Dictionary (1982)

1.2 A civic model of religion

All these characteristics can be traced to a cultural model shared by most of the cities of the ancient world, whether Greek, Italic or Roman. In this world, religion was linked with the ideal of the city that had been developing in the Mediterranean since the eighth century BC. According to this ideal, which was celebrated by Greek and Roman orators and thinkers and was also implicitly recognised by religious practice, the liberty of the citizen overrode all other considerations even in relations with the gods. That, at least, was the ideal proclaimed by the civic religion: it respected the liberty of the citizen and helped him to establish relations with the gods that were founded upon reason rather than fear.

As a result of Roman imperialism and the progressive extension of Roman citizenship, the Roman religious system was constantly expanding, and the number of religions practised in Rome and by Roman citizens everywhere increased. Traditional religion became more complex but without losing its traditional character. However, that character began to change as the old Mediterranean ideal of the city evolved, making possible other types of relations between citizens on the one hand and between men and the gods on the other. These relations were no longer based on the principle of the citizen's liberty but rather on absolute submission to some authority and to a master. The pace and the extension of that evolution varied from one place to another and from one period to another. Certain individuals and groups had long been seen as excessively religious (or 'superstitious', as the Romans termed it), putting themselves blindly and absolutely in the control of their gods. But it is fair to say that in was only in the third century AD that this attitude began to make itself strongly felt and to spread widely, affecting traditional circles as well as groups won over by Christian preaching.

2 CONCEPTS

Many Latin terms can be misleading, for the concepts that they cover are not the same as those to which they have come to refer in modern languages. To avoid anachronisms and to grasp the status of the religious in Roman culture, it is essential to understand these terms.

2.1 Religion, superstition

2.1.1 Religio

Ancients writers appealed to two different etymologies to express what they meant by the term *religio*, whose translation is always a delicate matter. Sometimes they traced the word back to *religare* ('to bind'), sometimes to *relegere* ('to pick up again', 'to go back over'; also with the sense of 'religious scruple'). In the first case, their intention was to underline the links between men and the gods, in the second it was to emphasise the need for scrupulous observance of religious obligations. Religion as a communal relationship with the gods, and religion as a system of obligations stemming from that relationship, were, for the Romans, the two principal aspects covered by the term *religio*, the one being, as it were, the corollary of the other. At any rate, *religio* designated not any direct, personal, sentimental link between an individual and a deity, but rather a set of formal, objective rules, bequeathed by tradition. It was within the framework of those traditional rules and that system of 'etiquette' that an individual established a relationship with the gods. Actually, another way of defining *religio* was to describe it as 'the pious cult of the gods' (Cicero, *On the Nature of the Gods*, 1.117). This point of view is slightly different, but the general meaning remains the same: religion consists in 'cultivating' the correct form of 'social' relations with the gods, essentially by celebrating the rituals implied by the links that exist between the gods and men. According to Cicero, relations with the gods took place within the framework of two ritual categories, the *sacra* (principally sacrifices, vows and rites of homage) and divination.

2.1.2 Superstitio

The term 'superstition', as traditionally defined, referred to a whole set of religious attitudes in the widest sense. Superstitious people thought that the gods were evil, jealous and tyrannical, and this distressed them. This 'ill-controlled fear' of the immortals drove them to all kinds of excesses, in particular to slavish forms of behaviour designed to win the favour of the gods. In contrast, the correct approach to religion involved believing that the gods were good and respected the social code of the city: so long as they were not gravely offended and the city institutions continued to function, the gods were not expected to take direct revenge or to heap disasters upon weak human beings. That was the gods' way of honouring the contract of respect and assistance that they were commonly believed to have made with Rome.

In the Christian period, *superstitio* acquired a complementary meaning. The term now designated the religion of a false god, that is to say of the pagan gods, who were regarded as demons. The meaning of the concept of 'religion' also changed: this now meant belief in the one true god.

2.2 Sacred, profane, holy

2.2.1 Sacer, sacrum

The term *sacer*, often misunderstood under the influence of primitivist theories, referred to ownership. 'All that is considered to be the property of the gods' was *sacer* (Macrobius, *Saturnalia*, 3.3.2, quoting the jurist Trebatius, a contemporary of Cicero). In other words, what was *sacer* was 'that which has been dedicated and consecrated to the gods' (according to another jurist, Aelius Gallus, also a contemporary of Cicero, in Festus, *De uerborum significatione*, p. 424, ed. Lindsay). The sacred was not, strictly speaking, a divine quality recognised to be possessed by a being or a thing. Rather, it was a quality that men ascribed to beings or things. The gods were not sacred, and (conversely) no object could be considered to be divine. The sacred was not a 'magic force' placed in an object, but simply a juridical quality possessed by that object. Like all public or private property, the property of the gods was inviolable, the more so because its owners were terribly superior to men and their vengeance was inexorable. The true meaning of sacrilege was infringement of divine property.

At the level of public cults, 'consecration' (the process of making something sacred) could only be carried out by magistrates or persons whom the law had charged with the task. In fact, in public cult, the only sacred buildings or objects were those consecrated by the supreme magistrates or by those elected by the assembly to do so in their name. Thus, despite the tolerance shown to private initiatives and the value that these might possess in the eyes of individuals, offerings made in an informal manner in sanctuaries or public spaces were not sacred and could be destroyed if the state judged this to be necessary. As we shall see, the quality of sacredness sometimes rested simply in its recognition by the proper authorities: that is to say, certain objects themselves signalled that they had been appropriated by the gods (for example, a place struck by lightning). Provided the correct forms were respected, a sacred object could always be rendered profane again, in other words withdrawn from the gods' property. This happened in the case of sacred spaces and, regularly, in the course of sacrifices.

One old Roman custom consisted in consecrating to the gods those guilty of certain crimes (*sacratio*). In the historical period, this was the punishment that those who broke vows called down upon their heads. Through this act of 'self-consecration', the individual became divine property. His exclusion was marked by his marginalisation in the city, the more so given that the *sacratio* frequently involved the deities of the underworld. Such an individual, now an object of horror, was considered to be so contemptible that, in this case, the term *sacer* gained a negative sense.

2.2.2 Profanus

Sacer was the opposite of two other qualities: *profanus* and *religiosus*. In principle, anything not sacred was profane (Paul Diaconus, Summary of Festus, *De uerborum significatione*, p. 257, ed. Lindsay), as were, more specifically, any sacred things that were ritually transferred to human beings (Trebatius, in Macrobius, *Saturnalia*, 3.3.4). The profane was thus an offshoot of the 'sacred', as we shall see in the case of sacrifice.

2.2.3 Religiosus

Technically speaking, this term designated objects or places marked by death: places struck by lightning, or tombs. The Romans thought that any place struck by lightning 'immediately became religious because some deity seemed to have dedicated it to himself' (Paul Diaconus, Summary of Festus, *De uerborum significatione*, p. 257, ed. Lindsay). Above all, however, the term *religiosus* was applied to 'places left to the *di manes*' ('gods of the departed': see below, Chapter 9) (Gaius, *Institutes*, 2, 4). In a broader sense, *religiosus* could also be applied to temples or to pious people.

2.2.4 Sanctus

Sanctus ('holy') was a term applied to anything which it was a religious offence to violate (Festus, *De uerborum significatione*, pp. 348, 420, ed. Lindsay). This category included city boundaries, certain laws, treaties, tribunes of the people, and official Roman ambassadors. Objects or persons who were 'holy' were neither sacred nor profane, but their integrity and security were guaranteed and confirmed by a sanction, itself instituted by an oath or, in particularly solemn circumstances, by a sacrifice that mimicked the expiatory killing of whoever did violence to the object or person in question. The sanction generally consisted in a *sacratio*, hence the expression *sacrosanctus*, 'sacrosanct, guaranteed by a *sacratio*'. *Sanctus* was applied to anything inviolable and therefore pure. It was a quality that could apply to tombs as well as to sacred objects and, in certain cases, to the deities themselves.

2.3 Piety, impiety

2.3.1 Pius, pietas

The term 'piety' has a wider sphere of reference than 'religion': it covered the correct relations with parents, friends and fellow-citizens as well as the correct attitude with regard to the gods. Piety functioned as a form of distributive justice, regulating men's obligations towards the gods. 'Piety is justice with regard to the gods', Cicero wrote (*On the Nature of the Gods*, 1.116). It was a reciprocal social virtue, for the gods also had to fulfil their obligations. Piety implied purity, which was essentially a bodily state not directly related to intentions or morality. A Roman was impure if there was mourning in the family, just as a temple, a grove, a priest or a magistrate became impure as soon as they came into contact with death and mourning. To recover their state of purity, the individual or sacred place had to undergo purificatory rites which ranged from ablutions or the sprinkling of water to periods of waiting, leading to a progressive return to a 'normal' state. That was why one would bathe before a sacrifice and wash one's hands before any religious action, even in the course of a complex ritual.

2.3.2 Impius, impietas

Impiety was the opposite of piety. It consisted in denying the gods the honours and rank that were rightfully theirs, or in damaging their property by theft (sacrilege, in the strict sense of the term) or by neglect. Impiety could be accidental (*imprudens*) or deliberate, with malicious intent (*prudens dolo malo*). If one accidentally disturbed the correct performance of a ritual or offended a deity out of ignorance and without meaning to do so, the impiety could be expiated by a sacrifice and possibly by making reparation for the wrong. But if the offence was deliberate, it was inexpiable. In this case, the community freed itself from the responsibility by an expiatory sacrifice and by making good the damage; but the guilty person remained forever impious and could never be expiated. On top of the punishments that the city could inflict on him for having violated public law and *sanctitas*, the impious offender was 'handed over' to the gods for them to 'do justice' for themselves.

Impiety according to the Romans

1. The principle

The praetor who has made a legal decision at such a time is freed of his sin by the sacrifice of an atonement victim, if he did it unintentionally; but if he made the pronouncement with a realisation of what he was doing, Quintus Mucius said that he could not in any way atone for his sin.

Varro, *On the Latin Language*, 6.30

If anyone violates (this prohibition), let him offer an expiatory sacrifice of an ox to Jupiter; if anyone violates (this prohibition) with intent, let him make expiatory sacrifice of an ox to Jupiter and let the fine be three hundred *asses*.

Spoleto ruling (*ILLRP*505)

When a sacrifice is committed, that which cannot be expiated remains inexpiable; that which can be expiated, let the public priests expiate it. The divine punishment for the perjurer is annihilation; the human punishment is infamy.

Cicero, *Laws*, 2.22

▶

▶ **2 The *exemplum***

Neither was his (Apollo's) son Aesculapius a less effective avenger of religion flouted, indignant that a grove consecrated to his temple had been in large part cut down by Antony's Prefect Turullius to make ships for his commander. But Antony's forces had been defeated even as the wicked work was in progress and the angry god, by the manifest power of his deity, drew Turullius (now condemned to death by Caesar's (i.e. Octavian's) order) into the grove that he had violated and thus brought to pass his execution by the Caesarean soldiers in that very spot.

Valerius Maximus, *Memorable Doings and Sayings*, 1.1.19

On impiety, see *Le Délit religieux dans la cité antique* (Coll. of the École Française de Rome, vol. 48), Rome, 1981.

3 A RELIGION RULED BY THE IDEAL OF LIBERTY

3.1 Liberty, the sole article of faith

A study of these key concepts gives a first impression of the fundamental representations that underpinned Roman religion. The principle by which it was ruled, in the historical period at least, was a civic rationality that guaranteed the liberty and dignity of its members both human and divine. That article of 'faith', virtually the only one known to Roman religion, was constantly affirmed and defended by authorities and thinkers alike. The traditional religion guaranteed the established order and ruled out any power founded upon fear. Relations with the gods were conducted under the sign of reason, not that of the irrational, in the same way as they were conducted between one citizen and another, or rather between clients and their patrons, but never between slaves and their masters.

In the name of that same principle, people could all honour the gods and practise whatever cults they chose, providing they respected the public cult and its pre-eminence, public order, and the liberty of others.

3.2 The limits of tolerance

The elite circles of society were nevertheless aware that this 'faith' in the liberty of bodies and minds was really an aspiration rather than a fact established once and for all. That is why they reacted, sometimes violently, when irrational anxieties and those who exploited them seemed to be carrying too much weight, as is shown by the Bacchanalia scandal (186 BC), by the numerous repressive measures taken against astrologers, charlatans and philosophers, and by the persecutions of Christians under the Empire.

Clearly this system and this 'faith' had the support of most Romans, so long as things went well and victories were the rule. But when, from the mid-third century AD onward, epidemics, invasions and internal rifts undermined that confidence in the city's ideological model, the old religion underwent a transformation and little by little was abandoned for another which seemed to offer more guarantees.

Chapter 3

Ritual and its formulations

The accounts of religious rituals, the debates of the Senate, the works of ancient poets and intellectuals, and even the myths of origins all tell us that the Roman religion was ritualistic. No modern historian has questioned this formalism. However, the rituals and the formalistic nature of the Roman religion have not been sufficiently studied. They are far from empty categories, and their performance and meaning play a central role in religious life and its interpretation.

1 TERMINOLOGY

1.1 Ritus

The term *ritus* (in Greek *nomos*) designated a mode of action, a mode of celebrating religious festivals or rituals, not the content of those festivals. To designate that content, that is to say what we now call 'rites' or 'rituals', the Romans employed the terms *sacra* or *caerimoniae*. A *ritus* was, on the other hand, a way of celebrating a traditional ritual – for example, a sacrifice: there was both a 'Greek rite' and a 'Roman rite'.

1.2 Caerimoniae

Rites and rituals, in the modern sense of the term, are complex sequences of actions and gestures that follow on, one after another, in a strict and progressive order. They are actions and gestures of everyday life whose primary meaning is known to all: greeting, honouring, giving, taking, receiving, dressing in a solemn fashion, behaving with humility; or else the opposite of all these.

Every ordinary Roman was capable of understanding the primary meaning of the rituals, particularly because, in his family, he himself would perform rites very similar to those celebrated in public places by magistrates and priests. And when ancient ritual forms, transmitted by tradition, gradually became obsolete, they were generally 'resemanticised' by those who celebrated them or by observers; the same was true for rituals imported from other cultures. So, for example, the reasons that learned Romans produced to explain why heads were covered during religious cult (see the text box below) are clearly reconstructions or rather erudite meditations on that ritual convention. These speculations are interesting in that they constitute evidence of the practice of ritual exegesis and reinterpretation, but in most cases they tell us nothing about the actual history of the ritual.

Clearly, a system of actions and rituals is comprehensible only in a particular setting, one that observes the same ritual conventions. So it is by no means certain that a stranger would have been able to grasp the primary meaning of certain Roman rituals without help from an interpreter, or that he would himself have been able to carry them out. It seems likely in the case of sacrifice that there was an elaborate and precise system of different actions and that only those who were native-born were capable of easily understanding them and executing them correctly. All the same, the major forms of prayer, of making offerings and expressing respect were more or less similar throughout the ancient world, so that 'translation' cannot have presented many problems. From this point of view, the public cult of Rome progressively came to constitute a bond between all citizens: this was their common tradition, whatever their origins and places of residence, a tradition proclaimed in stories, in images and in the commentaries of learned scholars. On the other hand, there were many differences between the cities of Italy and those of the Empire, and often even between cities that were close neighbours.

2 THE MEANING OF RITUAL ACTION

2.1 Actions that constituted implicit statements

Ritual gestures were organised in sequences that formed, as it were, propositions or implicit statements. For instance, during the immolation ceremony as carried out according to the 'Roman rite', the celebrant of the sacrifice sprinkled the victim's back with salted flour, poured a little wine on its forehead and ran a knife along its spine. Those three gestures effected a consecration, declaring that this victim, offered by the celebrants, had been transferred to the property of the deity. One of the most important of all ritual actions was speech. The prayer that necessarily accompanied the ritual conferred perfection and efficacy upon it. But the prayer added nothing new to the statement implied by the ritual, even if it sometimes made it less ambiguous. Speech was performative in that it 'realised' the gesture.

2.2 Rituals in their setting

The meaning of ritual actions could vary depending on their context; and 'second-order' meanings could be generated, to such an extent that they obliterated the primary, literal meaning. For instance, the calendar date chosen for a sacrifice or a dedication could steer its general significance in a particular direction, as could the cult setting in which a religious festival took place. The dynasts of the late Republic and, even more so, Augustus and his successors powerfully exploited every kind of external element in order to bring the meaning of religious festivals into line with their own projects. When restoring a temple, they would make the anniversary of the new dedication coincide with a date with a personal significance, for example Augustus' birthday (23 September), so giving the traditional festival of some deity a political meaning. Under Augustus, 23 September became the anniversary of the six temples situated in the area of the Circus Flaminius. The decoration of a sanctuary could, likewise, direct the thoughts of those present towards the glory of whoever had

had it built (examples that come to mind here are the temples of Venus Victrix in Pompey's theatre, or the colonnades surrounding the temple of Mars Ultor). From the beginning of the Empire in particular the strongly focused, axial layout of cult precincts acted to direct the thoughts of those celebrating the cult or engaging in other activities there. The Forum of Augustus alluded not only to the extinction of civil war but also to the redoubtable power of the man who had brought internal peace back to Rome. In other cases, it has been possible to detect allusions to philosophy among the decorative themes employed.

Examples of the decoding of ritual actions and gestures

1 Why do they bid the bride touch fire and water?

Is it that of these two, being reckoned as elements or first principles, fire is masculine and water feminine, and fire supplies the beginnings of motion and water the function of the subsistent element or the material?

Or is it because fire purifes and water cleanses, and a married woman must remain pure and clean?

Or is it that, just as fire without moisture is unsustaining and arid, and water without heat is unproductive and inactive, so also male and female apart from each other are inert, but their union in marriage produces the perfection of their life together?

Or is it that they must not desert each other, but must share together every sort of fortune, even if they are destined to have nothing other than fire and water to share with each other?

10 Why is it that when they worship the gods, they cover their heads, but when they meet any of their fellow-men worthy of honour, if they happen to have the toga over the head, they uncover?

This second fact seems to intensify the difficulty of the first. If then, the tale told of Aeneas is true, that, when Diomedes passed by, he covered his head and completed the sacrifice, it is reasonable and consistent with the covering of one's head in the presence of an enemy that men who meet good

▶

► men and their friends should uncover. In fact, the behaviour in regard to the gods is not properly related to this custom, but accidentally resembles it; and its observance has persisted since the days of Aeneas.

But if there is anything else to be said, consider whether it be not true that there is only one matter that needs investigation: why men cover their heads when they worship the gods; and the other follows from this. For if they uncover their heads in the presence of men more influential than they, it is not to invest these men with additional honour, but rather to avert from them the jealousy of the gods, that these men may not seem to demand the same honours as the gods, nor to tolerate an attention like that bestowed on the gods, nor to rejoice therein. But they thus worshipped the gods, humbling themselves by pulling the toga over their ears as a precaution lest any ill-omened and baleful sound from without should reach them while they were praying. That they were mightily vigilant in this matter is obvious from the fact that when they went forth for purposes of divination, they surrounded themselves with the clashing of bronze.

Or, as Castor states when he is trying to bring Roman customs into relation with Pythagorean doctrines: the Spirit within us entreats and supplicates the gods without, and thus symbolises by the covering of the head the covering and concealment of the soul by the body.

11 Why do they sacrifice to Saturn with the head uncovered?

Is it because Aeneas instituted the custom of covering the head, and the sacrifice to Saturn dates from long before that time?

Or is it that they cover the head before the heavenly deities, but they consider Saturn a god whose realm is beneath the earth? Or is it that no part of the Truth is covered or overshadowed, and the Romans consider Saturn the father of Truth?

Plutarch, *Roman Questions*, 1, 10, 11

2.3 The interpretation of rituals

There was nothing scandalous about giving a particular interpretion to a ritual so long as the ritual itself was not distorted or omitted. Whether it was celebrated fervently or with indifference, whether it was the sole focus of the action of a cult or was turned into just one element in a programme of political propaganda, made no difference to the ritual's intrinsic value. The only obligation that governed any individual ritual was that it had to be celebrated on a particular date and in the traditional order. There was no authority to prescribe the sense of the statement that it might be transmitting; so, since none was obligatory, one was as good as any other. Virtually the only limit to the semantic range of a ritual was the respect to be shown for the gods, at least near the temples where one communicated with them. Another limit was imposed by the traditional order of actions and attitudes, which immediately conveyed a literal meaning: sacrifice, for example, proclaimed the existence of the gods as partners of men in that they agreed to share a meal with them. But no one was obliged to give an account of the literal meaning of rituals.

As we discuss the evidence for rituals, we should therefore be careful to concentrate first and foremost upon precise information regarding actions and attitudes. We must note the spatial organisation of the cult place, the position of the celebrants in relation to the altar, their social rank, the articles that they handled, and then situate all this information within a physical, architectural context and within the framework of the calendar. What the celebrants thought, both during the festival and in general, may be of great importance to the history of thought and exegesis. But if we wish to study what was called religion in Rome, what we need to examine are the rituals themselves and their context. Likewise, we shall not be satisfied with the learned speculations of the ancients about which deity was involved with this or that ritual. To discover the theology behind the practice, we shall focus on the name of the deity, the deity's epithets, the objects surrounding the deity's religious image, and the ritual actions performed around it.

However, this way of proceeding will produce results only if we are careful to decode actions and attitudes within their context. We must always establish what a given physical gesture meant, in itself, in Rome, in such or such a period, before moving on to examine it within the wider system of ritual in order to determine its definitive meaning.

3 RITUS ROMANUS, RITUS GRAECUS

3.1 Categories that were complex and ambiguous

Sacrifices and other religious rituals were celebrated in accordance with either the *ritus Romanus* (the 'Roman rite') or the *ritus Graecus* (the 'Greek rite'). Those two forms applied only to public cults and they were, in fact, linked. The Roman rite was said to characterise traditional celebrations, the Greek to characterise cults imported to Rome from Greek lands. But those categories are complex. In the first place, there was no other kind of 'rite'. Attempts have been made to identify an 'Etruscan rite', in the account of the Secular Games (*Ludi saeculares*) of 204 AD, but the document is so damaged that the existence of any such ritual form is quite uncertain. Furthermore, the categories of the Roman rite and the Greek rite themselves do not seem to have been used before the third century BC, and cease to have been an important distinction by the end of the Republic.

It is important not to confuse the 'Greek rite' in the technical sense with all the foreign ceremonies imported into Rome during the last centuries of the Republic or to apply it to the cults of all the deities of Greek origin who were honoured in Rome. For the facts are not so simple. The cults of Aesculapius, Cybele and some aspects of the cult of Ceres, all imported from Greek lands, do not belong to the category of the 'Greek rite'. Rather, they are described as 'foreign cults', celebrated in accordance with the customs of their country of origin (*peregrina sacra*: Festus, *De uerborum significatione*, p. 268, ed. Lindsay). On the other hand, the cult of Hercules is classed under the Greek rite (though the cult of Castor and Pollux is not).

3.2 Definitions

These facts will suffice to suggest the particular character of these categories – categories which, in any case, were never systematically recommended by the Sibylline oracles. Upon closer examination, it becomes clear that the 'rite' is defined by certain features in the celebrant's behaviour. The Roman rite, which was according to myth established by Aeneas, consists in covering one's head when sacrificing and in preceding the sacrifice by a particular form of preliminary ritual, so as to effect a particular type of division of the victim (see below, Chapter 6). In the Greek rite, the heads of the celebrants were not veiled but crowned with laurel wreaths. It is generally believed that this ritual form was associated with a particular kind of musical accompaniment, hymns sung by choirs, the staging of *lectisternia*, and supplications. But there is no evidence to justify classifying these features as typical of the Greek rite alone.

3.3 The 'Greek rite', a very Roman ritual form

The truth is, the situation was more complicated than the simple polarity between 'Greek' and 'Roman' might imply. The cults performed according to the Greek rite in fact constituted an extremely *Roman* category that would certainly have seemed exotic to Greeks. Besides, we know that there was not *one single* Greek religion, but as many customs or religions as there were Greek cities. So whatever was the 'Greek rite' in question? In truth, it was an official category, more or less artificial, created by the Romans during the third and second centuries BC in order to give a name to certain new religious customs or certain old Roman cults whose Greek origins were now discovered or emphasised, such as the cult of Hercules. The same classification even covered the old Roman cult of Saturn.

In Rome and in the cities of Italy and Greece, the absorption of new deities and cults had been a constant feature for as long as could be remembered. It stemmed from the ability of ritualistic polytheism to innovate and to adapt representations to historical circumstances by 'naturalising' new gods and cults. So the Greek rite did not constitute a novelty by introducing Greek elements into the public religion. The term was designed rather to underline the presence of an extremely ancient Greek component in Roman religion than to mark a new phase in religious representations. It was partly by means of ritual that the Roman persuaded their neighbours and above all themselves that they had always been part of the 'Greek' world. On the basis of that claim they could integrate the cities of Magna Graecia and Sicily into the Empire and present themselves as the allies, interlocutors and (soon) 'natural' masters of the cities and kingdoms of the Hellenistic world.

3.4 Were those categories limited to Rome?

We do not know whether those ritual forms were also applied in the Roman colonies or whether they were adopted by the *municipia*. To be certain of that, we should need to know whether they applied to the semi-public cults in Rome itself: the cults at crossroads, the cults of colleges, and those of the army. As there is no positive evidence on this score, prudence dictates that the distinction between the 'Greek rite' and 'Roman rite' should be reserved for Rome's major public cults.

However, it seems reasonable to assume that all Roman religious groups in Rome, in the rest of Italy and in the provinces used analogous ritual forms. Categories of that kind made it possible for cities to commemorate their own religious traditions while at the same time affirming their Roman-ness. For that reason, it would be fascinating to obtain precise information about the sacrificial ritual of some city in Gaul, Syria or Africa.

Part II
Structures

Chapter 4

The division of time: calendars, rituals, regular festivals

One of the primary duties of the chief magistrates (*duouiri*) of a Roman colony – a duty taken over each year by their successors – was to define a public calendar. The inscribed charter of the colony of Roman citizens at Urso in Spain includes this clause:

> Whoever shall be *duouiri* after the foundation of the colony, they, within ten days next after that on which they shall have begun to hold that magistracy, are to raise with the decurions, when not less than two-thirds shall be present, which and how many days it may be agreed shall be festivals (*feriae*), which sacrifices shall be publicly performed (*publice*), and who shall perform those sacrifices. And whatever of those matters a majority of the decurions who shall then be present shall have decreed or decided, that is to be legal and binding and there are to be those sacrifices and those festival days in that colony.

Constitution of the Colonia Genetiva Iulia, of Urso, Baetica, article 64

1 THE ASTRONOMICAL CALENDAR AND THE CIVIC CALENDAR

1.1 There was no such thing as a universal religious calendar

The prescriptions laid down for the magistrates of Urso neatly encapsulate the particular nature of the Roman religious calendar. The first point to note is that there was no universal religious calendar. Each city, even a Roman colony, established its own, which did not necessarily mirror that of

Rome. Furthermore, the calendar was constructed not by priests, but by the leading magistrates in collaboration with the local senate. In Rome, the system was essentially no different, even if things were more complex: the calendar was, to be sure, managed by the priestly college of *pontifices*, but all decisions concerning the introduction of new festivals were dictated by laws passed in the assembly or by decrees of the Senate; and, according to myth, the major divisions of the year went right back to King Numa. The first consequence of this was that the official religious calendar of Rome or of any Roman city simply reflected the ruling of the authorities: and it mentioned only the regular major festival days. For this reason, the calendars inscribed on stone (known as *Fasti*) discovered in Italy and dating mainly from the Julio-Claudian period seem very 'incomplete' to our eyes. They include neither movable feasts nor ceremonies, sacrifices or public rites that do not correspond to the major festivals, nor the countless festival and cult days celebrated in the various sub-districts of the city, in colleges, in families or in other divisions of the Roman people. The fact nevertheless remains that the major traditional festivals do appear in these calendars, and that a major public deity was above all one who had received the privilege of an official festival day.

1.2 The natural calendar

After those preliminary remarks, let us now examine the general structure of the calendar itself. We need not dwell upon Roman traditions concerning the origin of the calendar: they are largely founded on the speculations and deductions of Roman antiquarians. All that needs to be said is that there were two types of calendar in the Roman world, one natural, universally recognised and accepted, and the other a civic calendar created by the city magistrates. The natural calendar was constructed according to the rising and setting of the signs of the zodiac, which determined in turn the sequence of agricultural labour on earth. The advantage of this calendar, often described as agrarian, is that it was to some extent universal, for it was the same for everyone. Through heavenly signs, it also represented a divine law for the pious to follow, since it appeared to rule agricultural labour and the cycle of plant growth. In the historical period this calendar was always part of daily life in the countryside, as well as being used in learned, astrological speculations. The second calendar, the civic one, was the calendar of magistrates and citizens.

The natural year according to Eudoxus of Cnidus (fourth century BC) and Varro (first century BC)

The Eudoxan calendar (a four-yearly cycle based on the twelve astronomical signs)

4 signs of 31 days + 6 signs of 30 days + 1 sign of 29 days + 1 sign of 32 days = 365 days.

The first year of the four-yearly cycle included one day added ('intercalated') at the end of the year. In this way, a sequence of four years of 365¼ days was obtained.

The Varronian calendar (derived from the Eudoxan calendar)

Sign	Date of rising	Length of month	Astronomical phenomena
Aries	17 March	31 days	24 March: New Year, spring equinox
Taurus	17 April	30 days	9 May: beginning of summer
Gemini	17 May	31 days	
Cancer	17 June	33 days	26 June: summer solstice
Leo	20 July	31 days	11 August: rising of the Dog Star, beginning of autumn
Virgo	20 August	30 days	
Libra	19 September	30 days	26 September: autumn equinox

▶

Sign	Date of rising	Length of month	Astronomical phenomena
Scorpio	19 October	30 days	10 November: beginning of winter
Sagittarius	18 November	29 days	
Capricorn	17 December	30 days	24 December: winter solstice
Aquarius	16 January	30 days	7 February: beginning of spring
Pisces	15 February	30 days	

1.3 The civic calendar

This calendar originally comprised 355 days: March, May, July and October each had 31 days, February had 28, the rest of the months had 29 days each. It is notorious for the problems posed by 'intercalation' up until the reforms of Caesar and Augustus. In order to keep it in step with the solar year of 365¼ days, every other year the pontiffs had to add 22 or 23 days (an 'intercalary month') after the day of the *Terminalia* (23 February), in other words between 23 and 24 February. As a result of neglect and manoeuvres by interested parties, the system went deeply awry. Despite a variety of adjustments, by the third century BC the natural, solar year and the civic year no longer corresponded. In 44 BC, the New Year (1 January) would have fallen on what was actually 14 October 45 according to the sun. In 46, at the instigation of Julius Caesar, the 'Julian' calendar system was instituted. Following one last correction in 8 BC, it functioned like the modern calendar, except that an intercalated day was added every four years not after 28 February but after 24 February. (In the Roman system it was the sixth day before the Kalends of March and so was called a 'double sixth' day, hence the term *bissextile*.)

The principal Roman civic calendars

The pre-Caesarean calendar

Year	Months × days	February (days)	Intercalary month (days)	Total (days)
1 Common	4 × 31 + 7 × 29	+ 28	–	355
2 Intercalary	4 × 31 + 7 × 29	+ 28	+ 23	378
3 Common	4 × 31 + 7 × 29	+ 28	–	355
4 Inrercalary	4 × 31 + 7 × 29	+ 28	+ 22	377
				1,465

In fact this gives a year of 366¼ days (to make it correct to the solar year, it would have been necessary to intercalate 21 and 20 days, which would have produced a sequence of four years with a total of 1,461 days, averaging a year of 365¼ days).

The Caesarean calendar

Year	Months × days	February (days)	Total (days)
1 Common	7 × 31 + 4 × 30	+ 28	365
2 Common	7 × 31 + 4 × 30	+ 28	365
3 Common	7 × 31 + 4 × 30	+ 28	365
4 Intercalary	7 × 31 + 4 × 30	+ 28	366
			1,461

That is, a year of 365¼ days.

2 THE STRUCTURE OF THE ROMAN MONTH

2.1 The division of days: the dies fasti *and the* dies nefasti

The first level of the organisation of the civic calendar concerned the general division of the days of the month. According to the encyclopedist Varro, a contemporary of Caesar, this division distinguished the days designated for the gods and those reserved for human beings: 'To the division made by nature there have been added the civic names for the days. First I shall give those which have been instituted for the sake of the gods, then those instituted for the sake of men' (Varro, *On the Latin Language*, 6.12). The idea was further developed by Macrobius (fifth century AD):

> Just as he had divided the year into months, Numa divided each month into days, which he distinguished by calling some festival days (*festi*), some working days (*profesti*), and some half-and-half days (*intercisi*). The festival days were consecrated to the gods, the working days were left to men for them to regulate their affairs both public and private, and the half-and-half days were common to both the gods and men. The festival days included sacrifices, sacred feasts, games and holidays; the working days comprised propitious days, *comitiae* days, and days suitable for the passing of a judgement; as for half-and-half days, each individual divides them up for himself, not in relation to the rest: for on those days, religion authorises the exercise of justice at certain hours and not at others.
>
> Macrobius, *Saturnalia*, 1. 16.2–3

The 235 or so days available for human action, known as *fasti* (marked as 'F' on painted or epigraphic calendars) were assigned to political business (for example, 192 of them were days when a public assembly, *comitia*, could meet: marked as 'C'), to juridical or military matters, to commercial business, and to work. The 109 days created in honour of the gods were called *nefasti* ('N' on the calendars); of these, a certain number – about 61 – were also designated as a public festival (*feria publica*, which is probably the significance of 'NP' on the calendars; it was only in the first century AD that days that were not public festivals in the traditional sense began to be designated feriae or 'holidays'). On days that were *nefasti*, the activities of mortals had to cease in public places, to make room for religious ceremonies that honoured the gods and celebrated their character and virtues. In short, the logic behind Varro's explanation of the division of the year is the idea that on the days devoted to them, the gods went symbolically about their functions, and that men honoured them because they did so in the interest of the whole community. An extra category was represented by the 'half-and-half days' (*intercisi*), during which some hours were reserved for the gods, others for human activities.

The balance between dies *fasti* and *nefasti* was variable. At the time of Caesar and, even more so, of Augustus, many official public festivals were created to commemorate their victories. Such decisions conferred upon Caesar and Augustus honours equal to those which the gods used to enjoy. And from the beginning of the Empire onward, many festivals were lengthened, in particular by extending their festive character to the days either side of the festival itself. On the other hand, the Saturnalia was celebrated for seven continuous days at the time of Cicero (from 13 to 23 December). It was officially reduced to three days under Augustus, but from Claudius onward again took up at least five days.

2.2 The regular proclamation of festivals

The *dies nefasti* included the Kalends (that is, the first of each month) and the Ides (which fell on either the 13th or the 15th, depending on the month). On the first day of the month a sacrifice was made to Juno, in the course of which Janus was invoked. Juno, supported by Janus, the god of beginnings, assisted in the 'birth' of the new month. The sacrifice was performed on the Capitol, in the *curia calabra*, by a minor pontiff who afterwards announced on what day the Nones of the month would occur (either the 5th or the 7th, depending on the month). On the same day, the *regina sacrorum* offered a sacrifice to Juno in the *regia*, in the Forum. On the day of the Nones, the *rex sacrorum* published an edict announcing all the regular fixed festivals (*feriae statae sollemnes*) up until the next Kalends. This ritual was still carried out at the end of the Republic and it shows that the actual calendar of days and festivals had to be set up by an edict published each month. It could not be established by edict once and for all. But the announcements of the *rex sacrorum* covered neither the movable feasts (*feriae conceptiuae*), which were announced by a magistrate (for example, the Compitalia, which were announced by the urban praetor), nor the religious rituals which did not count as major festivals and which were announced at the beginning of each year by the presidents of the priestly colleges or other sub-groups of the city.

3 THE STRUCTURE OF THE RELIGIOUS CALENDAR

3.1 The festivals of the 'calendar of Numa'

The traditional festivals that figure in the painted or epigraphic (inscribed) calendars fall into several distinct groups. The first is marked in large letters on the epigraphic calendars. Their names all have the same linguistic form (they are given as plural, in the neuter gender) and they go back to the earliest civic calendar, which was traditionally dated to the sixth century BC (the so-called 'calendar of Numa'). Although the date when this calendar was recorded in writing might be different from the date of its establishment as a system of festivals, it is reasonable to suppose that this was a set of extremely ancient festivals.

3.2 The agrarian cycle

In the civic calendar as we know it, several specific cycles of festivals are juxtaposed.

Agrarian festivals, through the homage paid to their patron deities, celebrated the seasonal sequence of labour and the submission of mortals to this fundamental law decided by the gods. It is easy to see that these 'extremely ancient' festivals were also festivals in the natural, cosmic calendar which had been transcribed into the civic calendar: here, their antiquity corresponded to the particular status of the 'natural' calendar established both before the city and outside the framework of civic religion. The reuse of this cycle may be interpreted as inscribing the natural rhythm of the year within civic time, in accordance with logic of civic life. The festivals in question were the following (note the -ia ending, as a neuter plural):

Cerealia (19 April), the growth of the cereals and other products of the fields
the first *Vinalia* (23 April), the opening of the jars of new wine
Robigalia (25 April), the warding off of wheat-rust
Lucaria (19 and 21 July/Quintilis), techniques of wood-clearance and the creation of clearings (?)
Neptunalia (23 July/Quintilis), controlling catchments of water and drainage
Furrinalia (25 July/Quintilis), finding underground water-courses and sinking wells
Portunalia (17 August/Sextilis), entering plots of land (in wagons?)
(Rustic) *Vinalia* (19 August/Sextilis), beginning the grape harvest
Consualia (21 August/Sextilis), storing the harvests
Volcanalia (23 August/Sextilis), fire prevention (in the storage chambers)
Opiconsiua (25 August/Sextilis), organising cereal reserves
Volturnalia (27 August/Sextilis), transporting produce along the Tiber (?)
Meditrinalia (11 October), sampling the new wine
Fontinalia (13 October), controlling natural water-courses and springs

Consualia (15 December), opening the grain-storage chambers
Opalia (19 December), abundant food supplies

You will have seen that some of these festivals celebrated the beginning of the cycle of food supply, others its conclusion. These may be complemented by the movable festivals of the *feriae Sementiuae* of late January (sowing) and the *Fornacalia* (completed on 17 February, involving the roasting of the cereals); and also by the sacrifice to Dea Dia, celebrated from 17 to 19 or 27 to 29 May under the Empire (when there was good light in the sky for the ripening of the crops). The cycle of festivals celebrating the achievement of farming also included a couple that related to stock-raising:

Fordicidia (15 April), the reproduction of the cattle herds
Parilia (21 April), the purification of the flocks of sheep and goats

3.3 The civic cycle

The first great cycle of 'natural' festivals, associated with the natural condition of mortals and the production of their foodstuffs in accordance with the law decided by the immortals, was matched by a second major group of essentially civic festivals:

Liberalia (17 March), linked in particular with the occasion on which young citizens adopted the adult dress of the toga
Quando rex comitiauit fas ('QRCF', literally 'when the king has held the *comitia*, the day is fastus', 24 March and 24 May), uncertain significance
Lemuria (9, 11 and 13 May), appeasing the wandering spirits of the unburied dead
Vestalia (9 June), the public hearth
Poplifugia (5 July/Quintilis), some connection with the people, but also uncertain

Saturnalia (17 December), a period of general 'partying', to celebrate the end of the year

Larentalia (23 December), uncertain; probably something to do with the underworld

Carmentalia (11 January and 15 January), knowing the right formulae for prayer

Lupercalia (15 February), 'chaos', representing the end of the year

Quirinalia (17 February), a festival relating to citizens

Feralia (21 February), festival of the dead

Terminalia (23 February), festival of boundaries and limits

Regifugium (24 February), uncertain (the official end of the year?)

It is interesting to note that the Romans celebrated two ends to the year. Up until 153 BC, 15 March served as the civic and religious New Year. This month more or less corresponded to the astronomical New Year. From 152 onward, the consuls took up their functions on 1 January, and on that account a number of festivals linked with the winter solstice and the broaching of stocks of food supplies became festivals marking the end of the year. The most famous of these was the Saturnalia, the central day of which fell on 17 December.

In addition to these civic festivals were others related to military life:

Equirria (27 February and 14 March), war-horses

Quinquatrus (19 March), the lustration of arms

and possibly also the *Tubilustrium* (23 March and 23 May, trumpets), and the *Armilustrium* (19 October). However, some aspects of these festivals are hard to understand. Jorg Rüpke has recently suggested that, rather than military festivals, they were connected to the actual structure of the month: like the Nones and the Ides, they were originally pivotal days in the second half of the month. Another ancient element in the calendar was the famous horse sacrifice

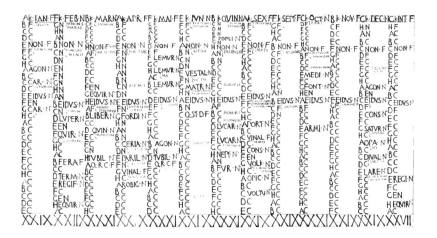

Figure 1 The pre-Caesarean calendar: the painted Fasti of Antium (84/
55 BC)

(known as the October Horse), on 15 October, which was
linked with the end of the season of war.

There were also the Roman Games (Ludi Romani) of 13
September and the Plebeian Games (Ludi Plebei) of 13
November, which dated back to the early Republic but only
later made their appearance on the calendar. These were
celebrated in honour of Jupiter and the Capitoline triad
(Jupiter, Juno and Minerva).

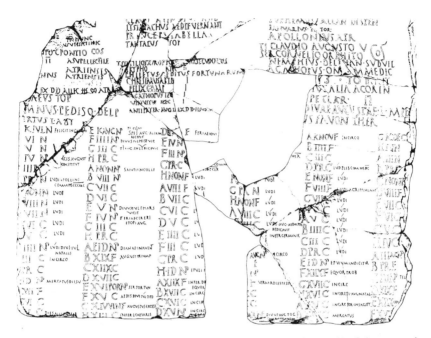

Figure 2 The Caesarean calender: the Fasti of the staff of Augustus' family (Antium, AD 23/37, fragment VIII)

3.4 Festivals linked to the structure of the year itself

Finally, some festivals celebrated the temporal structure of the year:

> *Matralia* (11 June), according to Georges Dumézil, linked to the summer solstice
> *Diualia* (21 December), linked to the winter solstice
> *Agonalia* (9 January; 17 March; 21 May; 11 December), the significance of which remains mysterious

There is no system which explains the order and the general characteristics of Roman festivals in the calendar, though some patterns can be detected. You will have noticed that most of these festivals fell on odd days in our calendar: the Feralia, for example, fell on 21 February, the ninth day before the Kalends of January. Frequently they are separated by an interval of one day and most fall after the Ides of the month concerned. In general, these festival days were work-free and included major sacrifices, sometimes linked with quaint rituals which, at the beginning of the common era, were seen as a sign of their antiquity. The extremely popular race of the *luperci* around the Palatine hill, on the day of the Lupercalia, was believed, for example, to go right back to Romulus and Remus. Most major festivals concluded with Games held in the Circus.

4 THE CREATION OF THE PUBLIC CALENDAR

This calendar seems to set out the city's essential activities and fundamental ideas: the construction of time, the beginning and end of the year and of the months, work in the fields which defined men's human (i.e. mortal) status, and the political and military functions through which the city fulfilled its destiny. In other words, it is tempting to see this programme of festivals as a rationalisation of existence typical of civic organisation and thinking, which took the place of the old 'natural' calendar.

4.1 The 'anti-priestly' calendar of the fifth century BC

However, we should always remember how little we know. Jorg Rüpke has recently shown that the public calendar was constructed in the fifth century BC, probably in the period of the *decemuiri* (451–449), in reaction against the religious power in the hands of the great families in the early city. Although it still does include quite a few of the old festivals, this official calendar was thus, in its origin, anything but 'religious'. If we study its internal logic in detail, we discover an underlying layer of reforms.

The initial intentions that guided the elaboration of this first calendar was different from the logic of the pontiffs: it was a matter of fixing the precise correspondences between the Kalends, the Nones, the Ides, and the days of the Roman 'week' (eight days, marked on the inscribed calendars with the first eight letters of the alphabet, A to H), quite independently of the religious reasons for dividing up the days. In this way, it was easy to calculate in advance when market days would fall (in principle, every eight days), without bothering about the intercalary month or the change of the year. It was at the end of the fourth century, in the context of the reforms of Appius Claudius, which affected the religious domain as well as the more strictly political, that another element in the public calendar was fixed: the announcement of which days were *fasti*, which *nefasti*. It is at this date that the names of the great public festivals seem to have found their way on to the public calendars. On the calendars of the late Republic, they are indicated in capital letters, in the same way as the principal divisions in the months (the Kalends, Nones and Ides). The names given to these festivals appear to correspond not to priestly terminology, but rather to the common language – another indication of the non-priestly origin of these documents.

Of course, that is not to say that a priestly calendar of festivals as such did not exist; rather, the calendar that resulted from the reforms of the early Republic and that is known to us through the Julio-Claudian inscriptions is a non-priestly document. As we have already seen, the festivals indicated in capital letters on the Fasti that we have represent no more than a representative selection of festivals. Many rituals and even major festivals do not appear at all on the Fasti: to name just a few, the spectacular celebration of October Horse on 15 October, which was linked in some way to the triumph of the early period and the end of the military year; the procession to the chapels of the Argei in mid-March; and the great ceremony for the fulfilment of the public vows undertaken for the wellbeing of the Republic on 15 March or, later, on 1 January. It is thus important to distinguish between the public calendar, with its own particular conventions and choices, and the religious calendar proper, as announced and observed by the priests, magistrates and college presidents. The latter calendar was not affected by the creation of the public calendar, whose primary aim was to fix and publicise the system of days meant for civic affairs.

4.2 From a functional register to the celebration of victorious generals and emperors

From the second century BC on, calendars listed the days of the 'week', the days that were *fasti* and those that were *nefasti*, the divisions of the month, and the old festivals, and they were beginning to indicate, in small or red letters, the anniversaries of the principal temples and other religious events. This change goes back to Fulvius Nobilior, who had the first calendar of this type displayed in the temple of Hercules of the Muses, which had been consecrated between 180 and 170 BC. Temple anniversaries constituted, according to Jorg Rüpke, the main reason for the introduction (or perhaps reintroduction) of fuller religious information in the calendar of the second century BC: it was a way for *imperatores* to write their own history into the calendar, at the same time as that of Rome. Quite apart from their religious significance in the structuring of the year, the ancient Roman festivals – or so learned antiquarians understood – did indeed trace the very history of Rome. For those writers, the old rituals invoked Romulus, Numa, the expulsion of the kings, and (in the case of the Plebeian Games, for example) political events; so too did the anniversaries of famous temples (the Capitoline triad, Castores, Ceres, Liber, Libera, Fortuna muliebris, etc.). But from the end of the third century and especially the beginning of the second, the constructions and reconstructions of temples at the hands of victorious generals reached such a point that the architectural scenery of the city was transformed. The anniversaries of these new, restored or reconstructed temples did of course celebrate the victories of the Roman people, but equally commemorated the triumphs of the great families.

5 WHAT THE PUBLIC CALENDARS DO NOT SAY

We must conclude from this that the 'real' Roman religious calendar cannot be reduced to the documents that we call Fasti. No document of the type that we might imagine exists.

If it did, it would certainly include public festivals, but also countless private festivals and rites. At the public level, apart from the major festivals on public holidays, whether fixed or movable, the anniversaries of the founding of temples, and the Games and other rituals connected with the worship of the gods, it would have to mention the consultation of auspices, the pronouncement of regular vows (on 15 March or 1 January under the Republic, 1 and 3 January under the Empire) or extraordinary ones, sacrifices to give thanks to the gods, expiatory sacrifices and supplications. And that would still not suffice. It would also be necessary to incorporate the calendars of families, the army, the colleges of merchants, artisans and other sub-groups of the city, and those of Roman colonies and *municipia*, not forgetting those of foreigners. It is not hard to see why no calendar registered such a welter of festivals and ritual obligations.

Moreover, the obligations that official calendars did register by no means applied to everybody either in Rome or in the *municipia* and the colonies. Many festivals and rites concerned above all the magistrates and public priests, and in many cases only some of those. For most ordinary citizens the effect of the great festivals was largely negative or passive: they could not take action in the courts or conclude any legally valid business, or work in any of the public areas of their city. Apart from that, they could attend the rituals as spectators, try to take part in a distribution of sacrificial meat, or perhaps watch the Games held during major festivals. But that was a right, not a duty. On the other hand, everybody, citizens and non-citizens alike, took an active part in the religious festivals and obligations that concerned them within the context of domestic cult or of the religion of smaller, local communities within the city.

It would be mistaken to transpose that typically Roman calendar just as it stands to other cities. The constitution of the Colonia Genetiva, cited above, stipulates no festivals other than that of the Capitoline triad, the equivalent of the Roman Games in Rome (13 September) and, given the date of its creation, that of Caesar's own 'dynastic' deity, Venus. Everything else is left to the free choice of the local authorities. Elsewhere, the constitution (article 92) of the Flavian *municipium* of Irni, in Baetica, mentions among the days when justice is suspended the festival days (*festi dies*) during which the imperial family is worshipped and a number of festival days (*feriae*) that seem to be an assortment of ancient community festivals.

It is clear that colonies and *municipia* did all adopt the Roman civic calendar with its divisions of the months and the year. The local Italian calendars and names of months disappeared in the course of the first century BC, and there were similar developments in the westernmost part of the Empire. However, the 'foreign' cities of the Greek-speaking parts of the Empire (cities of *peregrini*, those who were not Roman citizens) kept their own calendars, and only a few adjustments involving the names of the months or the fixing of the New Year modified the existing rules (as in the province of Asia, for example, at the beginning of the common era).

It nevertheless seems likely that the major towns outside Rome (particularly those that had some Roman status, such as colonies or *municipia*) adopted part of the festive calendar of Rome. But in all likelihood what this involved would have been the festivals and rituals connected with a particular deity or temple and the new festivals of the imperial house, rather than Rome's whole cycle of traditional festivals. The old festivals and likewise the system of distinguishing days as *fasti* and *nefasti* only really concerned Rome and Roman citizens as such. If they lived far from the capital, the ancient festivals of the Roman people affected them in a general cultural sense perhaps, but directly only if they actually visited Rome. It is also likely that local calendars developed more or less everywhere, in particular from the beginning of the Empire on, when the world's cities were progressively integrated into the Roman system. In truth, even in cities that had adopted the Julian months and years, lists of religious rituals (*feralia*) existed alongside the official calendars that were displayed in public places. Cities probably put on a public display at more or less the same traditional Fasti as Rome itself, but also observed a series of local festivals. Lists of such festivals could just as well emanate from the cities themselves as from the sub-groups within them. We know, for instance, of the recommendations of article 64 of the Constitution of the Colonia Genetiva, quoted at the beginning of this chapter, and also of the Feriale Duranum of Dura-Europos, on the Euphrates (third century AD); the former reflected the religious duties of the colony, the latter those of a cohort of Roman army auxiliaries.

Chapter 5

The division of space: temples, sanctuaries and other sacred places

Just as the city extended its control to time, so also it defined and controlled space. You could say that the city arranged the division of space between men and gods.

1 INAUGURATED PLACES: THE *TEMPLUM*

The space occupied by the city was 'liberated and pronounced to be designated' (*liberatus et effatus*). In the course of this operation, carried out by augurs, places destined to be appropriated by the city and its functions were freed from all divine constraints. Such was the case for the ancient territory of Rome (*ager Romanus antiquus*), the city itself (*urbs*) and the *templum*. These spaces could then be 'inaugurated' (*inaugurare*), meaning that they were defined with the approval of the auspices (on this concept, see below). Inauguration – or the definition of a space by the city with Jupiter's approval – was required for all public activities, or rather for all public decisions: *comitia*, sessions of the Senate, judicial activities, places of cult activity, places where auspices were taken. Certain priests, such as the *flamines maiores*, the *rex sacrorum* and the *salii* were also inaugurated. A place approved by the auspices was a *templum*. According to Paul Diaconus, it was 'defined and closed in such a way that it was open on one side only, with its corners solidly fixed in the ground' (Summary of Festus, *De uerborum significatione*, p. 146, ed. Lindsay). Inaugurated spaces, which were in principle quadrangular, were marked by a bronze star (Festus, *De uerborum significatione*, p. 470, ed. Lindsay) and bore the description *augustus*, 'august'. Like priests who had been inaugurated, these *templa* could later be 'exaugurated', that is to say disengaged from their intended purpose on behalf of the community that had been sanctioned by the auspices.

A *templum* in the Roman sense of the term was neither a building nor a sacred place. For a *templum* to become sacred, it had to be wholly or partly consecrated. As many temples (in our sense) were built within *templa* or even covering their exact area, these were also called *templa*, and in this way the term gradually acquired the current meaning of a religious building.

2 THE *POMERIUM*, A SPECIAL BOUNDARY

A second boundary separated the city of Rome (*urbs*) from its territory (*ager*): the *pomerium*. This boundary was established by the official foundation rite of the city. It was therefore a feature only of Rome and of ancient towns in Latium and the Roman colonies, and it is not correct to use the term for Roman towns of the imperial period (nor, of course, did any without any formal Roman status (peregrini) possess a *pomerium*).

A passage of Varro describes the operation of foundation:

Many founded towns in Latium by the Etruscan rite; that is, with a team of cattle, a bull and a cow on the inside, they ran a furrow around with a plough . . . that they might be fortified by a ditch and a wall. The place where they had ploughed up the earth they called a *fossa*, 'ditch', and the earth thrown inside it they called a *murus* 'wall'. The *orbis*, 'circle', which was made behind this was the beginning of the *urbs*, 'city'; because the circle was *post-murum*, 'behind the wall', it was called a *post-moerium*; it sets the limits for the taking of the auspices for the city. Stone markers of the *pomerium* stand both around Aricia and around Rome.

Varro, *On the Latin Language*, 5.143

Towns were positioned inside their *pomerium*, and its line ran inside a ditch and a rampart of earth. As André Magdelain has shown, the *urbs* was not itself a *templum*, even though the *pomerium* constituted the limit for urban auspices: the purpose of the *pomerium* was to mark and preserve the integrity of the ground set aside for the town's auspices, and to distinguish it from outside territory where the city's auspices could not legitimately be taken. But in order to take the auspices within the city, a *templum* had first to be marked out within this special, privileged space.

To preserve the integrity of the space within the *pomerium*, it was forbidden to place any tombs there; and the army, that is to say soldiers bearing arms, were not allowed to enter it (except during a triumph), no doubt because they were defiled by warfare, or rather because the *pomerium* marked out a sphere of different, civic (in our sense 'civilian') existence. It follows that the *comitia centuriata*, which was the assembly of citizens in their military capacity, could only be held outside the *pomerium*. The pomerial line consituted the boundary between the *imperium domi* (civic power, within the city) and the *imperium militiae* (full power vested in the armies, in other words outside Roman territory). Deities that presided over activities involving death and destruction, such as Mars and Vulcan, could not be given sanctuaries inside the *pomerium*. That did not prevent some places connected with the cults of such deities from surviving within the *pomerium* – trapped, as it were, by the later extension of the city boundaries. For example, the Volcanal in the Forum remained on the spot that it had occupied in the archaic period, but when a new temple to Vulcan was founded, this was positioned on the Campus Martius, on the other side of the *pomerium*.

At first sight, it seems that certain deities of foreign origin, such as Apollo (although he may well have been a warrior god initially), Hercules, Diana, Juno Regina and Aesculapius, may also have been relegated beyond the line of the *pomerium*. Was the pomerial space reserved for strictly Roman deities? The question is complex and much debated. The ambiguity of any such rule is illustrated by the fact that the Greek Castor and Pollux had their temple right in the middle of the Forum and the Great Mother was up on the Palatine. In any case, under the Empire, the rule no longer applied – even if it had earlier. The whole question was certainly more complex than Georg Wissowa (who proposed a sharp division between foreign and native deities) believed, and we cannot be certain that under the Republic deities of foreign origin were excluded from the *pomerium*. It was rather the hostile nature of the deities that really mattered – functional hostility such as that of Apollo or Hercules, or at any rate behaviour considered to be hostile to the Romans. Thus, at the beginning of the common era, Isis was banished from the area of the *pomerium* to more than a thousand paces beyond it because she had been the patron goddess of Egypt, the enemy of Octavian and the Romans.

The *pomerium*, as it is recorded in Roman myth, ran around the Palatine; under the Republic it corresponded more or less with the line marked out by the Servian wall of the city (established by the king Servius Tullius). The *pomerium* was directly linked to Roman imperial territory, because any general who had increased the latter also had the right of extending the *pomerium*. That was done several times during the Republic and Empire, and the *pomerium* ended up by incorporating a large part of the Campus Martius as well as the Aventine Hill.

3 SACRED SPACES

The space of the city and of its territory was divided between gods and men into spaces that were sacred and spaces that were not. There were two types of sacred spaces: those that men had dedicated to the gods and constructed for them; and those that the gods had somehow chosen and arranged for themselves, which men simply recognised rather than created.

3.1 Sacred places and objects

There were many kinds of sacred places constructed by men. They ranged from simple religious precincts equipped with an altar all the way to grand temples surrounded by colonnades that dominated a site with an altar and possibly also secondary buildings. In the eyes of the city, or from the public point of view, only spaces or buildings that had been legally consecrated were sacred. An altar or temple that had not been consecrated in the regular fashion, that is by a magistrate with *imperium* or a person legally charged to do so, was not sacred, but profane.

This does not mean that unofficial altars and chapels dedicated by private individuals in public spaces were systematically destroyed by the authorities. In general, such private dedications were tolerated, even though they did not enjoy the juridical status conferred by a regular consecration. That same principle also applied to all offerings made by private individuals in public sanctuaries. They could be placed in the public space, but if they were in the way they were summarily removed, for from a legal point of view they were not sacred. It is worth noting, however, that if there were too many such objects or if they had been damaged, they were usually buried within the sanctuary as if, after all, they were recognised as possessing an inalienability of the same type as that of sacred objects or, at a private level, of objects known as *religiosi*: they were protected and could not be alienated. They fell into the same category as tombs or places struck by lightning. Initially, the categories of *sacer* and *religiosus* were valid only in Rome itself and the territory of Rome. Only after the Social War were they extended to the whole of Italy. Though, in fact, in legal terms, even public dedications there were considered not 'sacred', but 'as if sacred' or 'as if religious' (*pro sacro, pro religioso*).

3.2 Consecration

Consecration was a complex operation. It was only possible on Roman territory that had been 'liberated and pronounced to be designated', and possibly inaugurated. After an official decision to proceed to a consecration (known as a *constitutio*), the space concerned was purified, the limits of the construction were marked, and the first stone was laid. Tacitus provides a good description of all this in his account of the purification and designation (by the sacrifice of a pig, a ram and a bull, called a *suouetaurilia*) of the site of the Capitoline temple, which had been destroyed by fire during the civil war of AD 69:

> On the twenty-first of June (AD 70), under a cloudless sky, the area that was dedicated to the temple was surrounded with fillets and garlands; soldiers who had auspicious names entered the enclosure, carrying boughs of good omen; then the Vestals, accompanied by boys and girls whose fathers and mothers were living, sprinkled the area with water drawn from fountains and streams. Next, Helvidius Priscus, the praetor, guided by the pontifex Plautius Aelianus, purified the area with the sacrifice of the *suouetaurilia*, and placed the vitals of the victims on an altar of turf; and then, after he had prayed to Jupiter, Juno, Minerva, and the gods who protect the empire to prosper this undertaking and by their divine assistance to raise again their home which the man's piety had begun, he touched the fillets with which the foundation stone was wound and the ropes entwined; at the same time the rest of the magistrates, the priests, senators and knights, and a great part of the people, putting forth their strength in one enthusiastic and joyful effort, dragged the huge stone to its place. A shower of gold and silver and of virgin ores, never smelted in any furnace, but in their natural state, was thrown everywhere into the foundations.
>
> Tacitus, *Histories*, 4.53

Once the construction was completed, it was dedicated or consecrated. The dedicant took hold of the door-jamb (or in the case of an altar, touched it) and, following the dictation of a pontiff, pronounced the dedicatory formula (*lex dedicationis*) which transferred both the building and the space from public property to the property of the gods: they were now sacred. The *lex dedicationis* also laid down a number of stipulations relating to the forms of the cult. Frequently, the dedicants would take as their model the *lex* pronounced on the occasion of the dedication of the altar of Diana on the Aventine (Dionysius of Halicarnassus, 4.26; *ILS,* 4907).

3.3 Terminology

Cult sites bore a variety of names, some of which are hard to understand. We have already noticed the ambiguity of the term *templum*, which designated sometimes an inaugurated space, sometimes a building, generally an inaugurated one. *Aedes* referred to a building in which a deity resided, and may be translated as 'temple'; *aedes* makes no reference to the status of the place where it is built and can also refer to non-inaugurated cult sites such as the *aedes* of Vesta. Most temples were of a quadrangular design but some, such as the sanctuary of Vesta, that of Hercules *oliuarius* in the Forum Boarium, and the Pantheon, were round.

Delubrum was the word for the paved area linked to a temple, a precinct surrounded by colonnades, or a temple. *Fanum* had a generic meaning and referred to either a cult site or a temple; though it was not a term frequently used. A *sacellum* was in principle a roofless consecrated place (an open area containing an altar; an altar outside a chapel or placed before a niche), whereas a *sacrarium* was a building in which sacred objects were stored.

3.4 The layout of cult places

A cult place was surrounded by a wall, railings or boundary stones. Its most important feature was the altar (*ara*), which was all that was essential to celebrate a cult: the most famous example is the Altar of Augustan Peace (Ara Pacis) on the Campus Martius in Rome. Sanctuaries at crossroads, in the various districts of Rome, consisted of an altar, possibly placed before a niche or a chapel, containing the statues of the Lares Augusti and of the genius ('spirit') of Augustus. Many places dedicated to the imperial cult were isolated

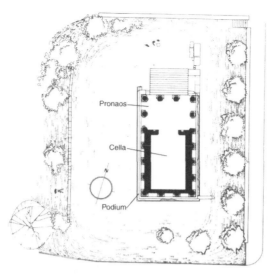

Figure 3 A Roman temple (from J.-P. Adam, *Le temple de Portunus au Forum Boarium*, Coll. of the École Française de Rome, vol. 199): ground plan

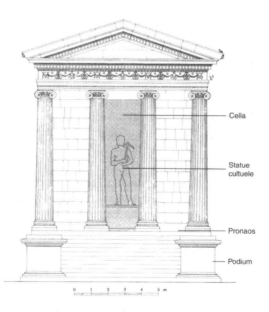

Figure 4 A Roman temple (from J.-P. Adam, *Le temple de Portunus au Forum Boarium*, Coll. of the École Française de Rome. vol. 199): facade

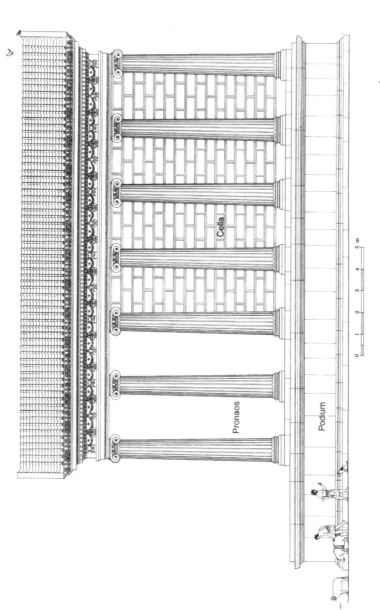

Figure 5 A Roman Temple (from J.-P. Adam, *Le temple de Portunus au Forum Boarium*, Coll. of the École Française de Rome, vol. 199): side view

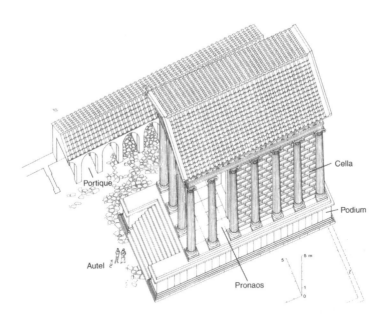

Figure 6   A Roman temple (from J.-P. Adam, *Le temple de Portunus au Forum Boarium*, Coll. of the École Française de Rome, vol. 199): axonometric plan

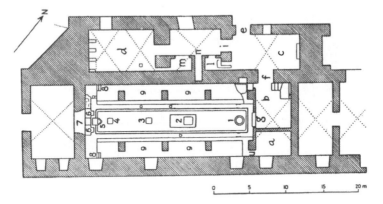

Figure 7   The Mithraeum of the Baths of Caracalla (from M. J. Vermaseren). a. Atrium. b. Atrium with a deep basin. c. Passage with a semi-circular tank. d. Room with a table, four semi-circular niches and an encircling ditch. e, f, g. Entrances. 1–4. Openings. 5. Triangular base. 6. Access to cult niche. 7. Cult niche. 8. Staircase leading to *triclinia*. 9. *Triclinia*. i. Passage.1–m. Small washrooms. n. Entrance to an underground passage. u. Entrance to a cult chamber.

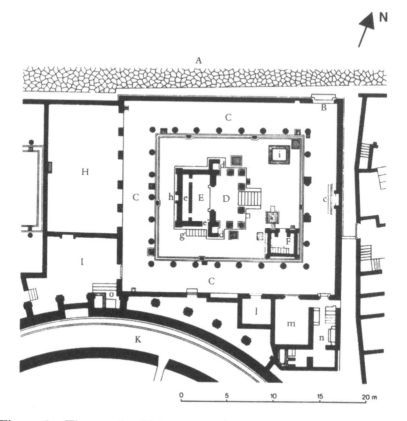

Figure 8   The temple of Isis at Pompei, AD 62 (from E. La Rocca, M.
and A. De Vos, *Guida archeologica di Pompei*)
A. Street. B. Entrance. C. Colonnade. c. Small chamber with
a wooden bench. D. Pronaos. d. Niches. E. Cella. e. Hollow
podium with two openings. e'. Door. g. Side staircase.
h. Niche containing statue of Bacchus. F. Washroom. i. Ditch
for rubbish. k. Principal altar. L–m. Living rooms. n. Room
with hearth. H. Meeting hall. I. Ceremonial hall. o. Small
extra room. K. Theatre.

altars (for example, the so-called Lyons altar of the three
Gauls) or placed before a niche sheltering the statue of a *diuus*
(a deified emperor) or the genius of the emperor. Where the
site included a temple, the altar was always positioned outside it, usually at its axis, except in the cult of Mithras, in
which the altar would be placed in an enclosed space representing a cave. Alongside the 'master altar', which belonged

to the deity who owned the temple, temporary altars (*temporales*) were often erected for 'guest' deities.

The temple itself was built on a raised podium, a typically Roman characteristic. A staircase led to the temple *pronaos* (porch), in which 'open-air' rituals were performed. At the back of the *pronaos* a doorway led to the *cella*, where the deity lived. Every deity was provided with a *cella* and an altar placed in front of the temple. The Capitol thus had three *cellae*, each with its own door: Jupiter's in the middle, Juno Regina's on his right, Minerva's on his left. At the back of the *cella* was the deity's cult statue. In many cases the *cella* contained a table (*mensa*) for extra sacrificial offerings, statues of other deities associated with the temple's titular god, works of art and ritual objects. Sometimes a secret place (known as an *adyton*) was constructed in the *cella*, to contain such objects. In principle, the *cella* was entered only for religious reasons, whether public or private. Some temples also had spaces about which little is known, designed to hold beds or chairs to accommodate the *lectisternia* and *sellisternia*. These were probably outside the temple.

In front of the temple, extending right round the altar and the *aedes*, was an area (*area*) the status of which might vary from one temple to another. In some cases it was sacred, like the temple itself, and could be entered only for religious reasons or for its upkeep. In others, part of it was profane, that is say accessible to the activities of mortals and for their offerings: *stelae*, altars and statues. The richest religious centres and those on their own in the countryside were in many cases flanked or surrounded by colonnades. These were designed to be used by human beings, who could shelter there from the sun or from storms. On a cult site situated on his land, Pliny distinguished between the *cella* of the temple and its colonnade as the difference between that which belonged to the deity and that which could be used by mortals: 'But there is no shelter near by from rain or sun, so I think it will be an act of generosity and piety alike to build as fine a temple as I can and add porticoes – the temple for the goddess and the porticoes for the public' (Pliny, *Letters*, 9.39.1–3).

Sometimes celebrants would hold banquets (particularly if, as sometimes happened, a number of rooms were attached) or would spend the night here. Many offerings and *ex-votos* were placed on show under the colonnades, and votive graffiti were frequently to be found even on the plastering covering their walls and columns. Sanctuaries outside the city, too far distant from Rome for the celebrants to return the same evening, were equipped with somewhere to stay (*hospitalia*), in some cases no more than a simple colonnade. Close to the temple or under the colonnade itself there would be a kitchen in which to prepare offerings and sacrificial banquets. Particularly well-equipped sanctuaries offered banqueting halls (*triclinia*). As constant ablutions were required in the performance of the cult, sanctuaries contained wells, pools and even, in the case of isolated sites, baths in which the celebrants could wash before the rites. Where protracted visits were necessary in sanctuaries situated some way out of town, these bathing establishments would offer the same services as the urban baths. Finally, some cult sites incorporated springs and pools and sometimes baths dedicated to a water deity, which were used for therapeutic purposes.

Depending on the requirements of the cult and the public activities that it involved, some temples had theatres or circuses associated with them. Major sacrifices would be rounded off by theatrical performances or chariot races. The tiered steps round these arenas where games took place could also be used for assemblies.

Some sanctuaries of Isis boasted, alongside a temple, representations of the Nile, such as the magnificent decorations of the Iseum in the Campus Martius, consisting of obelisks and sculptures in the Egyptian style, while others offered a simple room containing a pool of sacred water (as at Pompei, room F). Also attached would be somewhere to stay, somewhere for the priests or temple guests to gather (*pastophorion*), and somewhere for initiation ceremonies. Different again were the religious spaces devoted to other Eastern gods. Since the famous sanctuary of the Syrian gods on the Janiculan hill at Rome is currently being thoroughly reassessed, it is better to cite as examples the cult complex of Jupiter Dolichenus on the Aventine, dating from the second century AD, the Mithraic 'caves', and the premises devoted to the Phrygian cult in the Palatine temple of the Great Mother. A *mithraeum*, for example, generally situated below ground level, was shaped like an elongated *triclinium* at the end of which stood an altar and a bas-relief depicting the myth of the god.

The variety of settings was infinite, whatever the type of cult. But the Roman model of a cult place consists of an open area containing an altar, a temple and a number of chambers for various ritual functions. In private houses, the scale and number of cult places varied. Not all houses ran to a built-up or wooden *lararium* in the atrium or altars and extra rooms devoted to a cult as did grand aristocratic residences. In poorer houses, without an atrium or specially decorated rooms, the earthenware statuettes of the family 'pantheon' would be kept in cupboards, and sacrifices would generally be made on the ground or, when banquets were held, in the flames of a portable altar.

4 GROVES, CAVES, POOLS, SPRINGS

As well as spaces that were liberated, designated and consecrated, that is to say entirely arranged and controlled by the city authorities, there were natural places that the ancients considered to be residences that the gods had organised for themselves. These groves, huge caves, unfathomably deep pools and river sources inspired fear because they were used as places of residence by the gods. It was the terror and awe that such places inspired that signalled some divine presence. Mortals ventured to do no more than identify such spots and delimit them. They would enter them only to celebrate the cult or to see to the site's upkeep. Groves (*luci*) were particularly favoured by the gods as residences. Strictly speaking, a *lucus* was a clearing in a wood, and it would be in such a clearing, ritually cleared and tended, that the deity's cult would be celebrated. In some cases, temples and porticoes would be constructed there. Traditionally, the Latin League of the early Republic held its meetings in groves outside the towns, in Latium, for example, in the *lucus Ferentinae* or the *lucus* of Diana at Nemi, in the heart of the Alban Hills. Other groves, such as that at Feronia, twenty or so kilometres to the north of Rome (*lucus Feroniae*), later became the site of great fairs. After the Social War and the Civil Wars, some of these special Italic places were turned into prefectures or colonies in order to keep them under the strict control of the Romans (for example, Lucus Feroniae, the Lucus of Diana Tifatina, and the Lucus Angitiae).

Many of these 'natural' sanctuaries were situated in the territories of Rome or other cities, but some were to be found within the built-up area of towns. In Rome, for instance, the *lucus Vestae*, the *lucus Libitinae* and the *lucus Silvani* were all situated inside the city. Groves were not the only kind of sanctuaries to be found in the territories of Rome and other cities. As well as the suburban temples built very close to the *pomerium* and the town gates (for example, in Rome, the temples of Apollo, Hercules, Mars, Vulcan, and the sanctuaries of the Aventine), the territory contained temples way outside the city (extra-urban). Some of these were privately owned. Pliny the Younger writes:

> I must rebuild the temple of Ceres which stands on my property; it needs enlarging and improving, for it is certainly very old and too small considering how crowded it is on its special anniversary, when great crowds gather there from the whole district on 13 September and many ceremonies are performed and vows made and discharged.
>
> Pliny, *Letters*, 9.39.1–2

These cult places, constructed by local landowners or inhabitants, were used only by them. But the territory also contained extra-urban sanctuaries that were public and that should not be confused with the rustic cult places that were designed for the inhabitants of the countryside or as places of pilgrimage. Through the sanctuaries situated along the major roads and out near the edges of its territory, the city controlled the latter and celebrated that control. Those who visited such sanctuaries to celebrate the cult of a deity once or twice a year included city authorities, not just the peasants who cultivated the land around the sanctuary. The sanctuaries of the *uici* scattered across the territories of the major cities had a special role to play. Although linked to the community of the *uicani*, these cults were in fact public, for a *uicus* was considered a part of the city itself built in the outlying territory. So there was no difference between the cults of a *uicus* and those of a district of the city.

5 BURIAL GROUNDS AND TOMBS

Through the funerary rites, the dead, by some kind of apotheosis, joined the group of *di manes*. The tomb in which the remains of someone deceased were deposited was the place of a private cult managed by the family, and it belonged to the *di manes*, whose rights over that property were guaranteed by the city. All tombs, except those of newly born infants, had to be situated outside the *pomerium*. Usually cemeteries stretched along the roads leading away from towns or *uici*. In the city's territory, they were accommodated in the vicinity of farms. A tomb was a place strictly reserved for the dead and it could not be altered in any way without permission from the pontiffs. It was surrounded by facilities for the celebration of the cult or designed to increase prestige. The larger monuments comprised gardens situated inside the precinct, a *triclinium* for ritual banquets, and a special spot on the ground which was reserved for funerary sacrifices. Inscriptions inform us that such precincts offered places to accommodate all family members and friends. Because of the increasing shortage of space from the beginning of the

Empire on, the great families had underground cemeteries (catacombs) dug out of the tufa rock which formed the subsoil around Rome. These were collective tombs known in Latin as *columbaria* (dovecots), accommodating the urns of the dead in numerous niches. The dead from poorer families were buried in simple graves made out of masonry or dug in the ground and covered by tiles or half-amphoras. Amphora necks made it possible to communicate with the interior of a tomb and to pour libations into it. Nearby there would be pyres to be used for incineration. During the second century AD many tombs and mausoleums were modified in order to accommodate sarcophagi, for at this point the practice of inhumation (rather than cremation) became widespread again in Italy.

PART III
Religious Rituals

Chapter 6
Sacrifice

A sacrifice lay at the heart of most religious acts – so much so that Macrobius, in his commentary on Virgil, wrote that piety meant knowing how to sacrifice. There were dozens of ways of sacrificing correctly, depending on the type of sacrifice, the context, and the deity to be honoured. Incense might be involved, or some liquid, or plants or animal victims. But the forms of sacrifice did not depend solely on the social context or the deities concerned; they were also dictated by the ritual scenario of all the major religious festivals. The different kinds of sacrifices did not stand in opposition to one another; rather, they were complementary or differed in degree.

1 WHAT WAS A SACRIFICE?

1.1 Preparations, victims, offerings

A sacrifice was a complex rite that took place in an open space, in the presence of the community concerned. Within the framework of the public cult, it was celebrated in front of the temple, close to the altar set up in the religious precinct. Within a domestic framework, it took place on an altar, either fixed or movable, set up in one of the 'public' spaces of the house such as the atrium or the peristyle. Finally, private sacrifices connected with divination or magic were more likely to seek out isolated places, seldom visited – a quiet room, or a necropolis, for example. Sacrifices were offered by those who held authority in the community in question: the father of the family in a domestic context, the president (*magister*) in a college, the yearly magistrates or public priests in the city. But that authority could be delegated to substitutes. The celebrant of the sacrifice was assisted by attendants and slaves who were responsible for all the manual work entailed in the ritual. The evidence of Cato's treatise *On Agriculture* suggests that the form of sacrifice used in public cults and in the private cults of the leading Roman families was similar.

Both in public and in private religion, the ritual would usually start at the beginning of the day, at sunrise, close to the cult site (by contrast, sacrifices deemed to be 'magic' took place at night, in secret, avoiding any civic participation). First the celebrants and their assistants bathed or washed themselves. They wore special ceremonial robes. In the 'Roman rite', the official dress was the citizen's toga, draped in such a way as to leave the arms free and form a kind of hood or head-covering (the so-called *cinctus Gabinus*; literally, 'knotted in the Gabine fashion' – from the Italian town of Gabii). The animal victims, chosen (*probare*) to match the sex of the deity and in accordance with other ritual criteria, were always domesticated animals (cattle, sheep, pigs or occasionally goats). They were washed and adorned with ribbons and fillets of red and white wool. Their horns were gilded, sometimes decorated with discs (in the case of cattle); the backs of pigs and cattle were covered with a richly decorated, fringed blanket (*dorsuale*).

According to the 'Roman rite', male gods received castrated male victims (except Mars, Neptune, Janus and the *genius*, who were offered intact animals) and goddesses received female victims. Depending on the context, the age of the victim might vary, to express the hierarchy of a group of deities or that of the celebrants. In principle, adult animals (known as *maiores*) were deemed the more suitable for the public cult. Deities of the upper world received white victims, those of the lower world (such as Pluto) or those associated with the night received victims with dark coats. Vulcan and Robigo were offered red-haired animals. In certain sacrifices to Tellus or Ceres, pregnant cows were offered up. Pigs were generally used for expiations and for funerary cult. Other animals were used in certain special rites, a horse, for example, in the sacrifice of the October Horse (15 October), a dog in a sacrifice to Robigo (25 April), a white cockerel in the cult of Aesculapius. In a domestic context, other kinds of victims might be used, depending on the family's customs. Finally, in sacrifices involving magic, the ingredients varied depending on the purpose and the form of the ritual (the exotic regularly playing a part here).

Plant offerings were brought along in baskets, liquids in jugs, incense in small boxes. We do not know how vegetables were chosen or prepared. We do not even know exactly what was meant by *fruges* ('fruits of the earth'), a very common type of offering: was it a question of cereals or did fruits and vegetables need to be included? No doubt the precise meaning was determined by the context of the ritual. A list preserved by Festus (*De uerborum significatione*, p. 298, ed. Lindsay) mentions, as acceptable offerings in some context which is not exactly clear, 'a grain (*far*), boiled barley flour (*polenta*), leavened bread, dried figs, meat in the form of beef or lamb, cheeses, mutton, boiled grain (*alica*), sesame seeds and oil, scaly fish (except for *squatum*)'. Salted flour known as *mola salsa*, used constantly in public sacrifices, was prepared by the Vestals at the time of the Lupercalia (15 February), the Vestalia (9 June) and the Ides (13th) of September. But we do not know whether *mola salsa* was used in private sacrifices or in the colonies and *municipia*; and if it was, we have no idea who prepared it – whether the Vestals or someone else. In fact, virtually nothing is known about the forms of sacrifice in the colonies and the *municipia*. The suggestion that ritual was exactly the same there as in Rome is pure conjecture. The problem, in any case, is that there were no Vestals and no sanctuaries of Vesta outside Rome and Latium (where they were to be found in the cities of Lavinium and Alba, the legendary predecessors of Rome, as well as at Tibur).

1.2 Preliminary rites

Once preparations were completed, a procession moved towards the altar of the deity to be honoured. Surrounded by their assistants, the celebrants advanced to the altar. The sacrifice began to the strains of a flute. It started with the 'preface' (*praefatio*). The celebrant poured incense and wine into a fire burning in a round, portable hearth or brazier. The verb generally used for this is 'to do' (*facere, fieri*), for sacrifice is defined as an 'action' par excellence: literally, 'one *does* it with incense and wine, one *does* it with a victim'. The portable hearth used to transmit the offering to the deity in some way represents the identity of the celebrant, and so indicates what community is involved. We do not know what rituals were followed in the lighting of the altar fires. According to ancient sources, the goods offered (incense and wine 'unmixed', that is undiluted with water) were closely associated with the nature of the gods. Incense was supposed to represent their immortality and supremacy, while wine represented divine sovereignty. So through this *praefatio* the celebrants ritually proclaimed the immortality and superiority of the gods. In other words, this initial rite should be understood as a respectful salutation, acknowledging the principal qualities of the deities honoured.

In most cases the sources do not identify precisely which deities are honoured in the *praefatio*. In the prescriptions for sacrifice given by Cato, the *praefatio* is addressed to Jupiter, Janus and Vesta; in other cases it is clear that the particular deity to whom the sacrifice was directed was also included in the *praefatio*. This part of the ritual was in all likelihood addressed to all interested deities, from amongst whom the celebrants would sometimes single out one figure or another for special attention. At the same time, the *praefatio* presented the gods with, as it were, an invitation to the sacrifice. At Forum Clodii (Etruria), a religious rule dating from the beginning of the common era specifically declares that with this incense and wine the decurions 'invited to the banquet' the deities concerned (*ILS*, 154. 10–12). The *praefatio* thus constituted a summary of the rites that were to follow and explained their intention. On that account, it was a particularly popular subject for images of sacrifices and eventually came to signify, quite simply, *pietas*.

1.3 The immolatio: *consecrating the offering*

After the *praefatio*, the celebrant moved on to the immolation (*immolatio*) of the victim. In the Roman rite, he sprinkled the victim's back with salted flour (*mola salsa*, hence the term *immolatio*), poured a little wine on its brow, then ran the sacrificial knife along its spine. From the prayers of immolation and the commentaries of Roman antiquarians, we may conclude that the rite proclaimed the consecration of the victim. With the knife it symbolically transferred the victim from human property (the sprinkling of the *mola salsa*: flour was characteristically human food) to the god's property (the wine poured on to the animal's forehead). The action with the knife was, as it were, the verb in this proposition, in which the ritual flour represented the purity of the victim and its origin among human beings. Once that transfer was completed, the celebrant ordered a sacrificer to act (*agere*): this man struck down then bled large victims, such as cows or bulls; smaller animals had their throats cut. In principle, the victim had to indicate its consent, particularly by lowering its head. For this reason, it would generally be tied by a harness fastened to a ring at the foot of the altar so that, with a little help from the sacrificer, it would make the gesture of acquiescence. Any manifestation of fear or panic on the part of the victim was forbidden during the ceremony, as were all other disturbances. If any occurred, they constituted an unfavourable omen for the celebrant. In sacrifices conducted in accordance with the Greek rite, the celebrant, whose head would in this case be unveiled and crowned with a laurel wreath, scattered a few grains of wheat and drops of water on the victim's head, and then burned in the sacrificial fire a few hairs plucked from its brow.

Once slaughtered, the victim was laid on its back and cut open. With the help of his assistants, in particular the *haruspex*, the celebrant ascertained that the offering was accepted by the deity. Such acceptance (*litatio*) was indicated by the normal condition of the entrails (the *exta*, a group of five organs: the liver, the lungs, the gall bladder, the peritoneum and the heart). If these were all normal, it meant that the sacrifice was accepted and matters could proceed. If the *exta* showed any abnormality, the sacrifice was annulled. The entire operation was then started again from scratch, using different victims, and so it continued until the gods accepted it (*usque ad litationem*). In certain types of sacrifices, the *exta* were inspected, in accordance with Etruscan custom, with a view to telling the future (*haruspicatio*).

1.4 The sacrificial offering

At this point the victim was divided up. The portions belonging to the gods (the entrails, that is to say the seat of life) were set to cook in a pot in the case of bovine victims, or else grilled on skewers (sheep, pigs). When the boiling or grilling was completed, the celebrant tipped the deity's share, duly sprinkled with *mola salsa* and wine, into the sacrificial fire burning on the altar. Offerings to aquatic gods were tossed into water, those for chthonic deities (the Lares, for example) or deities of the underworld were thrown on to the ground or into a ditch, where they were burned. All these actions were accompanied by prayers which specified, without ambiguity, who was offering, who receiving, and who could expect to benefit from the ritual. In public sacrifices, the prayers always contained the formula 'for the Roman people' (Paul Diaconus, Summary of Festus, *De uerborum significatione*, p. 59, ed. Lindsay).

This description has reduced sacrifice to the bare essentials, but the rites themselves were frequently far more complicated than these basic actions. In the first place, the offering sometimes included other morsels of the victim's flesh: part of the offering might be cooked in a more elaborate fashion and then be placed, possibly in the form of meatballs, on a table inside the temple. Another variant of a great banquet for the gods was the ancient festival known as the *epulum Iouis*, the banquet of Jupiter on 13 September, at which senators feasted on the Capitol with Jupiter, and probably also with Juno and Minerva as well. This mode of celebration eventually became the general rule, and by the beginning of the common era a simplified form of *lectisternium*, involving a permanent display of couches (*puluinaria*), had been adopted by most public temples.

Thanks to the records of the Arval Brethren, we know that the god's banquet consisted – at least on some occasions – of two courses, just like a human feast: a meat course and a course of sweet wine and cakes. It was a kind of *symposium* during which the deity's statue was garlanded and perfumed. Throughout all the stages of these ceremonies, the human participants could, by actions and words, remind the deity of his or her functions and ask for favours. Add to this the fact that there was never just one deity in a cult place or a ritual, and that parts of the banquet, perhaps those that came from the subsidiary sacrifices (with victims of a lesser rank), were offered to the other gods and goddesses who were the 'guests' of the main patron deity of the cult site. All this makes clear that a sacrifice needed a good deal of time. The sheer complexity of the ritual meant that it took much longer than the brief formulae given in inscriptions or in ancient literature would often suggest.

1.5 The sacrificial banquet

When the offering had been consumed in the flames or placed on the ground, the rest of the victim was 'rendered profane', that is to say the celebrant 'seized' it by laying his hand upon it, thereby making it suitable for human consumption. The same procedure was followed with liquid offerings and probably also with those with those based on grain and vegetable (broths, cakes and breads). In this way, the celebrant did not consume sacred food but food that the deity had somehow agreed to let him have. This was far more akin to a gift (*sportula*) given to a client by his patron than to the incorporation of part of the deity by the faithful, as in the Christian Communion. It should be noted that in minor sacrifices offered in the course of large meals, it was the other way around: there, it was the gods who received a 'sportula' from the banquet host (see text box below).

An account of a public sacrifice: the sacrifice to Dea Dia (Rome, 17, 19 and 20 or 27, 29 and 30 May)

1. In AD 38

On the sixth day before the Kalends of June (27 May), Caius Caesar Augustus Germanicus, the president of the college of Arval Brethren, in his residence, which had belonged to his grandfather, Tiberius Caesar, b[egan] the sacrifice to Dea Dia in the open air, on the altar. Those present were Marcus Furius Camillus, Appius Iunius Silanus, Cnaeus Domitius Ahenobarbus, Paullus Fabius Persicus, Caius Caecina Largus, Taurus [Statilius] Corvinus, Lucius Annius Vinicianus, [Caius] Calpurnius Piso.

On the fourth day before the Kalends of June (29 May), in the sacred grove, the vice-president Taurus Statilius Corvinus, in the name of the college of the [Arval] Brethren, immolated a cow to Dea Dia. On the same day, at the same spot, Caius Caesar Augustus Germanicus, [president] of the college of the Arval Brethren, in the company of the flamen Appius Silanus, immolated a plump female lamb [to Dea Dia], and gave the signal to the four-horse chariots and the vaulting horsemen. Those present were Paullus Fabius Persicus, Cnaeus Domitius Ahenobarbus, Marcus Furius Camillus, Caius Caecina Largus, Lucius Annius Vinicianus, Caius Calpurnius Piso.

(The third day is not reported.)

2. In AD 87

(The ceremony of 17 May is not reported.)

In the consulate of Caius Bellicius Natalis Tebanianus and Caius Duce-nius Proculus, on the fourteenth day before the Kalends of June (19 May), in the sacred grove of Dea Dia, with Caius Iulius Silanus presiding and ▶

▶ Caius Nonius Bassus Salvius Liberalis officiating, the Arval Brethren celebrated the sacrifice to Dea Dia. Caius Salvius Liberalis, who was officiating in the place of the president Caius Iulius Silanus, in front of the sacred grove immolated on the altar two expiatory sows for the pruning of the sacred grove and the works to be done there; then he immolated a cow in homage to Dea Dia. Caius Salvius Liberalis Nonius Bassus, Lucius Maecius Postumus, Aulus Iulius Quadratus, Publius Sallustius Blaesus and Quintus Tillius Sassius seated themselves in the tetrastyle and consumed a sacrificial banquet. Each having donned a *toga praetexta* and a crown of wheat ears adorned with ribbons, they climbed the slope of the sacred grove of Dea Dia, after having dismissed their assistants, and through the medium of Caius Salvius Liberalis, who was officiating in the place of the president, and also through that of Quintus Tillius Sassius, who was officiating in the place of the *flamen*, they immolated a plump female lamb to Dea Dia; once the sacrifice was completed, they all made offerings of incense and wine. Then, having had the crowns carried into the sanctuary and having perfumed the statues, they elected Quintus Tillius Sassius as the annual president from the forthcoming Saturnalia until the next Saturnalia, and Celsus Marius Candidus as *flamen*. Then they descended to the tetrastyle, and reclining in the *triclinium* they banqueted with the president Caius Iulius Silanus. After the banquet, carrying the *ricinium*, sandals, and a crown of intertwined roses, and having dismissed the attendants, he (*sic*) climbed up beyond the barriers and gave the signal to the four-horse chariots and the vaulting horsemen. Under the presidency of Lucius Maecius Postumus, he (*sic*) decorated the victors with palms and silver crowns. On that same day those who had been present in the sacred grove dined in Rome with the president Caius Iulius Silanus at his home.

On the thirteenth day before the Kalends of June (20 May), the Arval Brethren dined with the president Caius Iulius Silanus at his home in order to conclude the sacrifice to Dea Dia. And in the middle of the banquet Caius Salvius Liberalis Nonius Bassus, Lucius Maecius Postumus, Aulus Iulius Quadratus, Publius Sallustius Blaesus, Quintus Tillius Sassius and Lucius Venuleius Apronianus made a sacrifice of incense and wine, assisted by the same boys, each with a living father and a living mother, as on the sixteenth day before the Kalends of June (17 May). And they had the offerings of cereals carried to the altar, touched the *tuscanicae* with flaming torches and made their assistants carry them to their homes. The boys [each with a living father and mother] who were present at the sacrifice to Dea Dia [were . . .]Ilius Marcianus, Publius Calvisius, the son of Ruso, [. . .] Marcus Petronius Cremutius, the son of Umbrinus [. . .]

3. In AD 240

On the sixth day before the Kalends of June (27 May), in the home of the vice-president Fabius Fortunatus, which is situated on the Capsaria street on the greater Aventine, [the vice-president] began the sacrifice to Dea Dia at sunrise; he touched fresh and dried cereals and loaves of bread surrounded by laurel leaves, and perfumed the goddess. Other priests, wearing the *toga praetexta* and fillets, in their turn sacrificed with incense and wine, touched fresh and dried cereals and loaves surrounded by laurel leaves, perfumed the goddess, sat down on chairs, and each received a *sportula* of one hundred *denarii*. Before midday, the vice-president, having bathed and donned a white dining costume, reclined on a couch and consumed the banquet. And the boys, sons of senators and each with a living father and mother, Lucius Alfenius Virius Iulianus and Lucius Alfenius Virius Avitianus, sat on chairs to eat and likewise consumed the banquet. After the meal, the table placed before the vice-president was removed. He washed his hands with water, a cover decorated with appliqué work was placed [on his couch] and he sacrificed with incense and wine, assisted by the boys, each clad in a *toga praetexta*, [who], together with public slaves, carried [the offerings] to the altar. The vice-president received a *sportula* and banqueting crowns [. . . *gap* . . .]

[On the fourth day before the Kalends of June (29 May), in the grove of Dea Dia, close to the altar, the vice-president Fabius Fortunatus Victorinus immolated two young sows to expiate the pruning of the sacred grove and the work to be done there; and there [he] immolated an honorific [cow] to Dea Dia; [then, having returned to the tetrastyle,] he sat down. [When he returned to the] altar he offered up to Dea Dia the entrails of the [two] young sows and, close to the silvered brazier, the entrails of the cow. He expressed [congratulations,] then, returning to the tetrastyle, he sat on the benches and ordered it to be noted in the *codex* that he had been present, had celebrated the sacrifice, and had offered up the entrails. He then laid aside the *toga praetexta* and went off to bathe. When he returned, he welcomed his colleagues, who were arriving. When the required number of colleagues had gathered, each laid aside his *toga praetexta*, sat down on the benches in the tetrastyle and had it noted in the *codex* that he had been present and had celebrated the sacrifice. Then a low table with no iron components was placed before them. They were served with bread rolls made from fine flour, consumed the 'black pudding' of the young sows, shared out [the meat from] them, and banqueted. They then veiled their heads in the tetrastyle and climbed up the slope of the sacred grove. The vice-president and the flamen sacrificed with pastries and griddle-cakes, immolated a plump, white, female lamb, inspected the entrails [to ascertain] the acceptance [of the goddess], and offered it as a sacrifice. They then ▶

▶ entered the sanctuary and, on a table on a grassy mound in front of [the statue of] Dea Dia, they each sacrificed three times on the table with three balls of liver bound together with milk and flour, then, in similar fashion, they each sacrificed twice on the earth with three more [balls] on the mound. Then having returned outside, close to the altar they prayed with the help of three balls of liver and three griddle-cakes. Re-entering [the sanctuary], they prayed again and touched the cooking pots with the boiled mixture. Then the vice-president, the *flamen* and the public slaves, and two priests were handed the cooking pots and, when the doors were opened for them, they cast the meal for the Mother of the Lares down the slope. Then, once the doors were closed, they sat down on the marble benches and shared the loaves made from fine flour and encircled with laurel leaves with their slaves and the rest of the staff. They then left the sanctuary and stood before the altar. The vice-president and the *flamen* sent two of their colleagues to fetch the cereals. When these returned with the cereals, the vice-president and the *flamen*, holding cups of wine, handed them over with their right hands and took the cereals in their left hands. Next, they recited a prayer and then, standing close to the altar, they all sacrificed with their boxes of incense and the cups of wine sweetened with milk. Then, with a basket, they sacrificed close to the altar with cakes as a form of contribution. They then re-entered the sanctuary, were handed the books and, striking the ground with a triple beat, they read out the hymn. At the given signal, they returned the books to the staff. They then perfumed the goddesses and offered lighted candles. The central door of the sanctuary of Dea Dia was opened and the crowns offered to Dea Dia were carried in, while Arescon Manilianus, the secretary, proclaimed the names of our Lord Gordian Augustus and those of the other priests. Next they read the book and elected (?) a president for the coming year, which [was to run] from the next Saturnalia [to the following Saturnalia] and proposed the name of the *flamen*. Congratulations followed and, each of them wearing a *toga praetexta*, they all descended from the sanctuary and entered into the 'pavilions' to change their garments. Having donned white outer garments and sheepskin sandals (?), [they moved] into the tetrast[yle] [. . . *gap* . . .].

(The account of the third day has not been preserved.)

Extracts from J. Scheid, *Commentarii fratrum arvalium qui supersunt: les copies épigraphiques des protocoles annuels de la confrérie arvale* (21 av.–304 apr. J.-C.), Rome, 1997 (pp. 28ff., no. 12; pp. 146ff., no. 55; pp. 331ff., no. 114).

Sacrificial victims offered to the deities of the underworld were completely incinerated (a holocaust), for the 'living' could not sit down at the table with gods who presided over the world of death. Sacrifices offered in a bid to gain influence over a deity often took the form of a holocaust, as these were generally addressed to gods of the underworld. Because people expected a specific result from these rituals, the offerings and the general context were somewhat different from the usual, everyday ones.

The consumption of portions of meat (accompanied by bread and diluted wine) or of liquids offered by the celebrant of a sacrifice is a complex problem, for the forms of this were legion. The only general principle governing sacrificial banquets was that of hierarchy and privilege. The celebrants and sacrificers generally consumed their portions on the spot, paid for by the community. In some festivals, particular social groups within the city banqueted at the public's expense (*publice*) at a specific cult site: so, for example, the senators ate on the Capitol on the occasions of the *Epulum Iouis*, the great sacrifice to the Capitoline triad on 13 September (the Ludi Romani) and 13 November (the Ludi Plebei). Under Augustus, they were granted the privilege of banqueting on all occasions at the expense of the people. Priests also enjoyed certain privileges, as did the Capitol's official flute players and probably also the *parasiti* of Apollo (theatre actors) in the temple of this god. These rules imply that not all citizens, not even all of those present at the sacrifice, took part in banquets at the people's expense. They probably had to buy their portions, either on the spot or at a butcher's shop, unless some benefactor offered to pay for their meat, along with the bread and wine that accompanied it. In any case, it seems that many public sacrifices produced no more than a limited banquet for the celebrants. The portions of meat that were left over were presumably sold in the butchers' shops to the other citizens. Following traditional Roman logic (as in the *census*, which gave greater voting power to the rich), the most eminent members of a group and those with authority always took precedence and received the best portions. All kinds of ways were found to satisfy the idea that public sacrifices were ostensibly offered for the Roman people as a whole: sometimes it was the people's representatives who banqueted, sometimes all the citizens who were present; sometimes – finally – all those prepared to buy the meat from a butcher. In smaller communities, at the level of a city district, a college or a family, the sacrifice and the banquet were more closely linked: those present consumed the sacrifice that they offered. All the same, the existence of numerous foundations set up by benefactors to finance the distribution of sacrificial meals suggests that normally the sacrificial meat was not shared out between all those present as a matter of course.

One particular, but very common, type of sacrifice was that offered during a public or private meal. In between the first course and the second, incense and wine would be offered up along with certain elements of the banquet and other specifically chosen offerings. This simpler form of sacrifice sometimes constituted the first or last phase in a major public sacrifice: it took place during the sacrificial banquet in the strict sense of the term. There can be no doubt that it constituted the most common ritual celebrated within a domestic framework. In all banquets, a sacrifice of this type was made to the Lares and the Penates and, from the end of the first century BC, also to the *genius* of Augustus. These sacrifices clearly underline the connection of the ritual with the practice of eating and feasting. During the offering the celebrants of the sacrifice would recline on dining couches (*triclinia*) and would share the food with the gods. In this variant of a sacrifice the mortals were the first to eat. This inevitably sets it apart from blood sacrifice, or at least from sacrifice celebrated in a sacred space, near an altar or a temple. If the sacrifice took place in a *triclinium*, in short in a human space, the mortals held the foremost role; if it took place inside the dwelling of a deity, the mortals waited respectfully for the 'owner' to consume his share, before appropriating the remainder of the offering.

Two private sacrifices (second century BC)

Before harvest the sacrifice of the *porca praecidanea* (offered before the harvest) should be offered in this manner: offer a sow as *porca praecidanea* to Ceres before harvesting spelt, barley, beans and rape seed; and address a prayer, with incense and wine, to Janus, Jupiter and Juno before offering the sow. Make an offering of cakes to Janus, with these words: 'Father Janus, in offering these cakes, I humbly beg that thou wilt be gracious and merciful to me and my children, my house and my household.' Then present the wine to Janus, saying: 'Father Janus, as I prayed humbly in offering the cakes, so wilt thou to the same end be honoured by this wine placed before thee.' And then pray to Jupiter thus: 'Jupiter, wilt thou deign to accept the cake; wilt thou deign to accept the wine placed before thee?' Then offer up the *porca praecidanea*. When the entrails have been removed, make an offering of cakes to Janus, with a prayer as before. After the same manner, also, offer wine to Janus and offer wine to Jupiter, as was directed before for the offering of the cakes, and the consecration of the cake. Afterwards offer entrails and wine to Ceres.

Cato, *On Agriculture*, 134

The offering is to be made in this way: offer to Jupiter Dapalis (of sacrifices) a cup of wine of any size you wish, observing the day as a holiday for the oxen, the teamsters and those who make the offering. In making the offering, use this formula: 'Jupiter Dapalis, for as much as it is fitting that a cup of wine be offered thee, in my house and in the midst of my people, for thy sacred feast; and to that end, be thou honoured by the offering of this food.' Wash the hands and then take the wine and say: 'Jupiter Dapalis, be thou honoured by the offering of thy feast.' Then, if you wish, make an offering to Vesta also. The feast of Jupiter consists of roasted meat and an urn (= 12.5 litres) of wine. Let the celebrant make the offering with ritual purity, and let him make it profane (= suitable for human consumption), by laying his hand upon it.

Cato, *On Agriculture*, 132

1.6 Other sacrificial rituals

At some specific rituals, such as the great *lectisternia*, all family heads would hold banquets, to which they invited all their neighbours and passers-by. It was a way of demonstrating the hospitality that they were offering to the gods, whether to thank or to appease them. Great sacrificial meals seem to have been the rule in the cult of Mithras under the Empire, for the Mithraic cult sites took the form of a large *triclinium* with an altar at one end. The initiates banqueted, and water, bread and wine were offered up; but we do not know when or how the blood sacrifice took place. As far as we can tell, some of the rituals celebrated on the occasion of the Megalesian Games in honour of the Great Mother (4– 10 April) consisted in private banquets. Leading families formed 'sodalities' to host lavish feasts known as *mutitationes* ('invitations to banquets financed in common'), no doubt in the company of the goddess, on the last day of the festival. This ritual calls to mind the hospitality that great patrician families offered to the Great Mother when she arrived in Rome in 204 BC. Alongside the *mutitationes*, the urban praetor offered up a public sacrifice. We know nothing, in the Republic at least (for later, see below), about the 'Phrygian' sacrifices made by the priests specifically attached to the goddess's cult.

As for the cult of Syrian gods, we know that this included sacrifices, but we have no information on their form. We may assume that they were subject to particular rules regarding purity. To judge by the equipment found in cult places of the goddess Isis, sacrifices did take place there; and we know of libations of water and offerings of incense. But the details of these rituals are unknown. In all imported cults such as these, the processions and the spectacular rites of ecstasy and self-mutilation are better attested in our sources than are the rituals of sacrifice, no doubt because these were not all that different in their practice from those in traditional Roman sacrifices.

2 THE MEANING OF SACRIFICE

2.1 How should sacrifice be understood?

A study of the rituals known to us (mostly public ones), ritual vocabulary, and remarks found in ancient literature make it clear that Roman sacrifice was first and foremost a banquet, quite literally. In Roman ritual, as in the sacrifices in the Greek world, to sacrifice was to eat with the gods. But the meal offered to the gods was more than a banquet. To sacrifice was – in the course of a feast to which the gods were invited – to divide the food into two parts, one for the deities, the other for the human beings. Through this division of food between the gods and the humans, sacrifice established and represented the superiority and immortality of the former, and the mortal condition and pious submission of the latter. The occasion was not placed under the sign of the terror inspired and exercised by the gods. The idea of human sacrifice was ruled out, even symbolically. The violence was discreetly done to a third party, an animal or a plant, and it represented a clear line in the hierarchy of beings. The gods and men were above the line which marked out peaceful relations with due regard for civic liberty. Below the line were beings that were similar but inferior, destined for servitude to, and use by, their superiors.

2.2 Variants and deviations

We may well wonder whether banquets played a role in Egyptian cults, but we know too little about them to be certain. The idea of Mithraic sacrifice, while clearly linked with the context of a banquet, was founded on other representations too, notably the images of Mithras' violent immolation of a bull; through these it is possible to analyse something of the ritual's significance. It seems likely that during the Empire in the Phrygian cult of the Great Mother, as well as in Syrian cults, sacrifice (particularly the distinctive ritual of the *taurobolium*) had other connotations, which involved the submission of the victim, in contrast to the consent of the animal that was central to the traditional ritual. The effect of this proliferation of variants and refinements in the context of Roman sacrifice was to emphasise the complex nature of the gods. For those who reflected on Roman religion as a whole, the rites of Mithras or of the Great

Mother, taken together with traditional Roman sacrifices, represented the two types of relations that could obtain between mortals and immortals.

We can also understand why 'magic' sacrifices aroused hostility: not only were they believed to inflict physical or material damage on others, for the benefit of those who celebrated them, but they set out to subject a deity and, in many cases, a fellow-citizen to the will of the celebrant or his client. Such conduct flouted the principle of civic liberty and fell into the category of crimes of violence. A 'gentler' ritual, favoured by some philosophers, consisted in seeking particularly privileged relations with the deities (this was known as 'theurgy'). In principle, this ritual was not classified as violent, but the dividing line between speculation and transgressive behaviour was a tenuous one, and theurgy was viewed with just as much suspicion as 'magic'.

Human sacrifice was not altogether unknown in Rome. While opposed to this practice, which seems to have been performed sporadically up until the time of Pliny the Elder, the Romans did nevertheless describe as public sacrifices the burial alive of a pair of Gauls and a pair of Greeks, in the Forum Boarium. This was an exceptional ritual to which they resorted in periods of danger; through it they offered representatives of the enemies of the Roman people to the deities of the underworld. In similar fashion, the Romans would solemnly dedicate besieged towns to the gods of the underworld or, at the private level, their own personal enemies, using magical rites. These examples show clearly that the Romans did on occasion resort to the sacrifice of human beings, in order to shift the emphasis in relations between mortals and immortals by granting the immortals absolute power over mortals other than the Romans themselves.

2.3 Sacrifice, a 'credo' expressed by action

The kernel of the rite of sacrifice may be seen as a 'credo' expressed in action rather than words. This 'credo' was neither explicit nor prior to the ritual action itself: it was rather inherent in the ritual and proclaimed solely through a sequence of ritual actions. The only things prescribed were the order of these rituals and their permanence. So, for example, the ritual of the *praefatio*, which was repeated at the beginning of every new ritual sequence, had to follow a precise order of actions, but it was not necessary for the celebrants and those attending to be aware of its 'meaning' or explicitly to formulate in their own minds the salutation and homage that the ritual expressed. And the prayers that accompanied the actions of the *praefatio* added nothing to the homage expressed by the rituals. The division of food and the banquet that followed the slaughter of the victim, and the libation also, in their turn, proclaimed the 'credo'. The parts of the sacrificed animal that fell, as of right, to the god were the vital organs. Furthermore, the deity was privileged to be the first to 'banquet'; at least that was the case in actual cult sites (see above). In sacrifices involving liquids and plants too, that precedence granted to the gods drew a distinction between the immortals and the mortals. The secondary distribution of offerings 'made profane' (see above) similarly established and reflected the social hierarchy among the celebrants and others present.

3 ADDITIONAL FACTORS

Sacrifice was central to all major ritual celebrations. But, as we have seen, it took many different forms and was, furthermore, combined with a wide variety of intentions and contexts. Traditional Roman sacrifice did not commemorate any particular event (in the way that Mithraic sacrifice did or a Christian Mass does). It did not symbolise total abandonment to the deity or aspire to incorporate the god. Sacrifice was a banquet which offered men the possibility of meeting their divine partners, of defining their respective qualitites and status, and of dealing together with business that needed to be done. For example, human beings could make the most of this meeting to make their excuses for any deliberate or unavoidable infringement of the deity's property or dignity (with an expiatory sacrifice), to present a request or to convey thanks (through supplications or prayers for mercy), or to conclude contracts (with vows). Sacrifice thus constituted the culminating point in a widely diverse range of celebrations. Although sacrifice always affirmed the superiority and immortality of the gods and also their friendship towards humans, this 'credo' took on particular meanings according to the context. That explains why sacrifice was central to the regular festivals in the calendar. The anniversary of the foundation of a temple began with a sacrifice; complex and picturesque rites in the contexts of one or more sacrifices could proclaim the function of a deity and ask him or her to discharge it with generosity. Certain major rituals, such as the regular vows at the beginning of the year, great festivals such as the Roman Games of 13 September and the Plebeian Games of 13 November, extraordinary ceremonies such as those involving vows, triumphs, *lectisternia*, dedications, purifications and the Secular Games all featured sacrifices or often even culminated with them. Within the space of this book, it is not possible to describe all the rituals that provided a setting for Roman sacrifices. Detailed descriptions can be found in encyclopedias and larger textbooks. We shall simply consider briefly the major categories of celebrations that included one or more sacrifices. But first, a few words on the ritual of prayer and sacrificial offerings.

3.1 Prayer

We have already mentioned the language of action, which finds its full expression in sacrifice and its wider ritual context. But very little has been said about the words, the prayer (*precatio*), that accompanied sacrifice and all other rituals.

Prayer was closely linked to ritual. It was an indispensable element in ritual and – vice versa – there was no praying without ritual. Prayers were recited while a celebrant performed the prescribed actions: like the instruments of sacrifice, prayer served as a means of celebrating the rite.

Inseparable from action, prayer was superimposed upon it; it said in words what the body of the celebrant conveyed by its actions. Prayers were often formulated as imperatives and were to be understood as official instructions, conveyed in the plain language of Roman magistrates.

Prayer was performative. Whereas actions were not strictly supervised and could be repeated, if incorrect, at the cost of an expiatory sacrifice (*piaculum*), prayers were closely monitored, for they could not be repeated or corrected. Once pronounced, they produced their effect, for better or for worse. That is why those who pronounced the prayers read out the most important of them from texts or had them dictated by an assistant (*praeire in uerbis* or *uerba praeire*). A gesture could be ambiguous: for example, the act of touching could be interpreted in many different ways. But speech was not ambiguous; it was precise. So celebrants accordingly had to take great care over the names of the deities they invoked and of those who were to be beneficiaries of the ritual, as well as over the exact formulation of what they wanted. These precautions were particularly important in rites designed to force a deity to render a specific service. 'Sorcerors' claimed that they knew the 'true' secret names of the deities and could use them to ensure that the rites were effective. These are the exotic, barbarian names that appear on curse tablets and on magical papyri. But similar precautions were also taken in the most official form of cult. The tradition that Rome itself had a secret name, which was supposed to protect the city against an *euocatio* (Pliny the Elder, *Natural History*, 28.18; Plutarch, *Roman Questions*, 61) may be of late date and simply speculation on the part of antiquarians, but it certainly refers to the hold one could gain over a deity if one knew his or her real name. In that case prayer was guaranteed to be effective. Despite their importance, however, prayers were not superior to actions. They were the equivalent of the latter and their necessary complement, and vice versa. The function of prayer was not to provide a metaphysical or spiritual basis for ritual. It was not designed to explain it. It simply expressed it in words and, by making it explicit, conferred a formal perfection upon it.

Some rituals involved the recitation of hymns (*carmen*), which in some cases were sung to a musical accompaniment. This practice was adopted in traditional rites such as the processions of *salii* and the sacrifice to Dea Dia, in expiatory ceremonies recommended by the Sibylline oracles or in conclusion to the Secular Games. Hymns, whether of ancient or more recent origin, were not, strictly speaking, prayers. Rather, they were works of art designed to give pleasure to the deities, much as the Games did. They also differed from prayers in that they were frequently addressed to several gods at once, included mythological and exegetic elements, and were not so much precise as pleasing. A prayer, in contrast, could never be addressed to more than one god and never contained any commentary on any kind of rite: it was an act, not an ornament. A hymn, for its part, would be composed by a poet (in 17 BC the hymn for the Secular Games was composed by Horace), and would not be repeated from traditional texts controlled by the priests. A hymn was designed to win the gods over by the aesthetic and intellectual pleasure that it afforded them. It constituted an ornament added to the rite, but unlike prayer was not a necessary element in it. In fact, the recitation of a hymn constituted a rite in itself, in the same way as supplications or the Games did.

3.2 Offerings

Relations between mortals and immortals were founded upon the exchange of gifts and counter-gifts. Sacrifice, which organised an exchange of offerings in the form of food and homage, fell into this category but was not the only means of maintaining those relations. At every level of society, individuals and communities offered gifts to the gods: there were gifts from the fathers of families, gifts from children when they passed into adulthood (the first beard, *bulla*, dolls and toys), gifts from the city, gifts from the senate and from individual military units, gifts from one of the tribes of the Roman people or from a college, and so on. The objects offered ranged from temples to small cult accessories and statuettes in wax or earthenware. Offerings are wrongly lumped together and all called *ex-votos* by modern scholars, for only some of them properly qualify for such a description. Many of these objects were given as tokens of thanks, or to conciliate a god or pay homage rather than in the fulfilment of a vow (which is what *ex-voto* strictly means). Besides, the little earthenware or wooden offerings in many cases were not the essential part of the gift that was made. Often they acted as a sign that a ritual had been completed, and that ritual was usually a sacrifice. These so-called 'ex-votos' were far more numerous than is generally believed, for small tablets or inscriptions on wood, objects made of wood or wax, placards, graffiti and objects in bronze and precious metals, which commemorated exchanges effected between mortals and some deity, have often vanished leaving hardly a trace. Small offerings themselves were regularly representations of the beneficiaries of the ritual: statuettes of those who said prayers, of *matronae* (that is to say, women who had had children: we should take care not to describe these statuettes automatically as 'mother-goddesses'), of children, as well as busts of men and women. Other objects allude to what was at issue in the ritual concerned: physical organs and limbs refer to a cure or perhaps to a successful birth or to fertility. But it would be over-hasty to conclude that these representations of organs and limbs always referred to rituals of healing, for some are ambiguous. If we study the *ex-voto* offerings that are explained by an accompanying inscription, we sometimes discover that feet may refer to a journey, a two-way journey (two pairs of feet, pointing in contrary directions), possibly a visit to a cult site. Ears may refer either to a cure or to a deity's granting of a request, or possibly to both. Hands may sometimes represent mutual trust and confidence (*fides*). Other examples certainly did commemorate cures or at least the preservation of health, a successful birth or a desire for children.

There were also many flasks of perfume, jars of wine, receptacles containing offerings of foodstuffs, representations of sacrificial victims, and altars both large and small, which referred more directly to the sacrificial context of the exchange. Finally, in some cases statues of gods, large or small, were offered to the deity who was to be honoured. They did not necessarily represent the deity to whom the temple was dedicated, so it is always risky to identify the temple's main god or goddess from the evidence of just a single statuette. All these objects could be fashioned either life-size or on a small scale – a choice that was not necessarily an indication of the social rank of the person sponsoring the dedication. The custom of depositing objects, whether or not strictly 'votive', in religious places dated from the archaic period. Very common in central Italy and Etruria from the fourth to the second century BC, offerings of model organs and limbs and earthenware statuettes disappeared at the end of the second century AD; the practice reappeared in the provinces of Gaul under the Empire.

Public offerings were consecrated. By an act of dedication, as described above, they became the property of the gods. Inscriptions spell out this fact, but often they do no more than simply mention the word *sacrum*, 'consecrated'. This word also appears on private offerings but, as we have seen, in that case it is not enough to make the objects legally consecrated; the authorities behaved *as though they had been consecrated*, and allowed them to remain where they had been left so long as they did not get in the way of the regular cult. The same principle applied to official consecrations made outside the *ager Romanus* and, after the Social War, outside Italy. If the offerings became too numerous or old and dilapidated, they were tidied away into suitable buildings or into storage containers within the sacred domain.

3.3 Vows

Many offerings and dedications, and also sacrifices and Games, were occasioned by public or private vows. A vow was a contract concluded with a deity. The settlement of a vow was conditional (see below); it sometimes, but not always, fell on a fixed date. One of the regular days for vows to be honoured corresponded to the New Year. Under the Republic, on 15 March, and after 153 BC on 1 January, the two consuls honoured the regular vows to the Capitoline triad and to Salus publica for the wellbeing of the Roman people, and pronounced new ones. This vow consisted in sacrifices. Jupiter received an ox, the three goddesses cows. Sometimes gifts made of precious metals accompanied the sacrifices, which, as may be imagined, were acts of solemn homage. This ceremony opened the civic year; that is to say, the first public act of the New Year was to recognise the honouring of the vows made the previous year by the consuls and the Senate, gathered together at the Capitol. Once the responsibilities of the magistrates at home and overseas had been defined, the consuls formulated the vows for the coming year. From the Empire onward a second vow was added, the vow for the health of the emperor and his family. After various experiments through the early decades of the Empire, in the reign of Tiberius the ceremony was fixed to 3 January. In Rome, public vows were pronounced by the consuls, but under the Empire, on 3 January colleges of priests and probably many other social groups also pronounced vows for the emperor's health. The same happened in the colonies, the *municipia* and the foreign (*peregrini*) cities of the empire. This ceremony developed into one of the greatest festivals of the year, while the traditional feast of the Kalends of January became an essentially private celebration.

We also know that regular vows were pronounced every five years by the censors, and that, as they left Rome, consuls and legates departing on military campaigns made vows for victory and a safe journey and return. In private life too, many vows were made. During temple festivals such as that of the temple of Ceres, on 13 September, which is described by Pliny the Younger (*Letters*, 9.39.2), vows, to be fulfilled on a fixed date, were concluded between the temple's titular deity and private individuals. But most vows were to do with the hazards of human life. Both public and private vows were devised for cases of sickness, travel, expectation or risk, and also for whole periods of life (childhood, for instance). The consuls formulated many special ('extraordinary') vows in the light of events as they occurred, particularly during the perils of war. Under the Republic, these extraordinary public vows were always formulated for the Roman people and in its name. This meant that, for the vow to be valid, it had to be approved by the Senate; otherwise only its author was bound by it. Many Roman temples were built as a result of this type of vow. Under the Empire, however, military dangers related above all to the emperor, who, in the name of the people, was in command of the so-called 'armed' provinces. That is why all the extraordinary vows known for this period are concerned with the success of the ruler.

Both regular and extraordinary vows were conditional. In other words, so long as the request had not been granted by the deity, the author of the vow was not obliged to discharge it. Thus, the famous vow of the *uer sacrum* ('consecrated spring') of 217 BC covered a period of five years and depended on victory for the Romans. As circumstances in 212 did not at all match up to the terms of the votive contract, the honouring of the vow was deferred. Livy, whose account is very precise, does not even mention the suspension of the vow's execution. That only arose in 195, twenty-two years later. At that point, with the conditions finally satisfied, the vow was immediately discharged. The vow of the 'consecrated spring' was of a particular type, perhaps borrowed from the Italic people, but subsequently adapted by the Romans. It involved the consecration of all the animals that would be born during the spring of the year when the honouring of the vow fell due. Because this vow affected not the property of the Roman people, that is, the state, but that of all Romans, the Senate ruled that it should be pronounced by all the citizens, gathered together in the Forum.

Other examples of annulled vows are attested under the Empire. When Emperor Titus died in September AD 81, the fulfilment of the vows made for his health on the previous 3 January were never again mentioned by the Arval Brethren. They were now content simply to 'commend' (*commendare*) once more the health of Domitian to the Capitoline triad and Salus publica. In other words, the vows for Titus lapsed and the priests confirmed the vows pronounced for Domitian Caesar on the previous 3 January, pointing out his change of status: for now he had become Domitian Augustus. Two other attested examples date from the Principate of Trajan. On 3 January 101 and 105, the Arvals ordered it to be noted in their records that on that date new vows were pronounced but no sacrifice was made. This was their way of saying that, at this time when the security of the Empire and the emperor were gravely threatened on the Danube, the conditions of the vows formulated in 100 and 104 had not been fulfilled. So the vows were no longer valid. There can be no doubt that these spectacular deferrals not only won support but also favoured the political propaganda of the imperial house. It is not hard to see why the exact terms of votive contracts were always carefully checked and recorded. Public vows were noted down in the records of magistrates and priests, and were announced in public under dictation by a colleague. Private vows were recorded on tablets that were sometimes posted up at a cult site, or even deposited at the foot of the god's statue. Many containers that originally held the seals of votive tablets have been found at cult sites. It is not hard to appreciate the legal importance of an offering made *ex-voto* in the strict sense of the term: it attested before all and sundry that the contractual obligation had been carried out by the appointed date. At the same time, the *ex-voto* celebrated the power and *pietas* of the deity so honoured.

There were several special types of vows. The ancient public ritual of *euocatio* involved luring the enemy god or gods into the Roman camp during a siege by vowing to set up a residence and a cult for them among the Romans.

According to tradition, Juno Regina of the Aventine had been 'evoked' in this way from Veii. The same ritual was employed in 146 in the siege of Carthage, and an inscription recently discovered in Turkey formally attests its use there in the first century BC.

3.4 Deuotio, defixio, sacratio

A ritual even more aggressive than *evocatio* was that of the *deuotio* of enemies. *Deuotio* was used in both public and private life. Generals, for example, sometimes vowed enemy troops to Tellus and the *di manes*; antiquarians preserved a formula that was supposed to have devoted the Carthaginians and their territory to Veiovis, Dispater and the *di manes* during the siege of 146 BC. A spectacular variant of the same ritual consisted in including a Roman or even oneself in the vow and then seeking death in battle: particularly renowned in Roman tradition was the *deuotio* of two members of the Decii family (Livy, 8.6.9f.; 10.8f.; but the tradition that involves a third Decius carrying out the ritual is doubtful). By devoting living beings to chthonic deities and the gods of the underworld, one consigned them to death, for it was expected that the deities in question would hear the vow and appropriate the persons consecrated to them. The terms of the contract were that the gods accepted the lives of the persons consecrated to them and, in return, wiped out the Romans' enemies.

The *deuotio* and its variant, the *defixio*, were frequently used in private life to vow personal enemies or rivals to the gods of the underworld. The votive 'contract' was inscribed on a small lead tablet which was then buried in a tomb so that the interested parties, that is the *di manes*, could read it and pass on the message to the gods of the underworld. Germanicus' death in AD 19 was attributed to a *deuotio* (Tacitus, *Annals*, 2.69), and countless such tablets have been found in the tombs and cult sites of the Roman world. In some cases the tablets (*lamellae*) were rolled up and pierced by a nail, seemingly the better to 'fix' the enemy. But devotions were not always addressed to the underworld gods. Any deity could be the beneficiary of one. It was, for example, quite common to devote a stolen or lost object to a deity so as to turn it into a sacred object and call down divine vengeance upon the thief.

When a solemn treaty (*foedus*) was concluded or a *clarigatio* (a claim for reparation) was made, a fetial priest called on Jupiter, Mars and Quirinus to witness it, and 'devoted' his own person and the Roman people in the event of the commitment being broken. Similar formulae were used when oaths were sworn. But in the case of oaths it was a matter not of a vow but rather of a conditional consecration (*sacratio*) similar to that which, ever since the archaic period, struck those who violated certain laws. A man who was *sacer* and so belonged to the deities to whom he was consecrated was nevertheless not supposed to be simply killed out of hand. However, if he was, the man responsible was not considered a murderer. *Deuotio* to the gods of the upper world is also attested by curse or binding tablets (*defixiones*) discovered in cult sites and by 'self-devotions' for the wellbeing of the emperor. The memory of this practice was preserved by the later formula '*devoted* to his power and dignity' (*deuotus numini maiestatique eius*).

All these practices show that there was no gulf separating religion and 'magic', just a difference of degree. Devotions could be applied to the officiant himself or to enemies of the Roman people without attracting criticism. Quite the reverse: such rituals were counted among the exemplary traditions of Rome. However, when they were directed against fellow-citizens they were condemned. So it was the intention and the application that rendered the ritual criminal, not the practice itself, unless it was also linked to the violation of a tomb.

4 GAMES

The great sacrificial rituals often included Games (*ludi*), whether in the form of theatrical shows (*ludi scaenici*) or

circus games (*ludi circenses*). In principle these Games concluded the sacrifices that were celebrated during festivals –
festivals which in many cases were named after the Games in
question. At the Roman Games and the Plebeian Games, the
Epulum Iouis, the great sacrificial banquet of 13 September
and 13 November, formed the heart of the festival. In the
historical period, the *epulum* was preceded by nine days of
theatrical Games and followed by four days of chariot racing
in the Circus Maximus – the Roman and the Plebeian
Games proper falling, respectively, on 15 September and
15 November. Other spectacles were added as extra acts of
homage. On the day of the Games, the statues of the Capitoline triad were carried in procession to the circus, where they
watched the races along with the Romans, in a space designed
'to bring the gods and men together' (Livy, 2.37.9).

The magistrates presiding over the games (who, in the
Roman and the Plebeian Games, would be the curule or the
plebeian aediles) wore the garments of a *triumphator*, which
suggests that these solemn Games were derived from the
ancient triumph. Before they became permanent fixtures,
most of these spectacles had originally been votive and linked
with victories. The number of days that they lasted at Rome
was constantly being extended. Despite repeated interven-
tions to reduce them, for example by Nerva (Dio Cassius,
68.2.3), in the reign of Marcus Aurelius they numbered as
many as 135. And on top of that figure we need to take
account of a number of days of Games that were repeated
(*instaurati*) thanks to an omission or mistake in the ritual.

The chariot races also featured vaulting riders (*desultores*)
who leapt from one horse to another. From the second
century BC on, these races were frequently followed by
running races and wrestling and boxing matches. From
186 BC (when the votive games of M. Fulvius Nobilior were
held), there are also mentions of hunts (*uenationes*). All these
spectacles complemented the programme of the traditional
games. An innovation of the Empire were the special
competitions (*agones*), which included gymnastics, poetry

(*mousikoi*) and horsemanship. As a rule, these *agones* took place every five years. The best-known was the competition founded by Domitian in honour of Capitoline Jupiter (*agon Capitolinus*), for which a stadium was constructed underneath the present-day Piazza Navona, as well as an odeon. Although some hunts and athletic competitions were included in the programme of the traditional Games from the end of the Republic on, gladiatorial fights were not. Along with hunts, these constituted separate spectacles (*munera*). Originally these contests took place in the course of private games offered on the occasions of funerals. They are first attested in Rome in 264 BC. One hundred and fifty years later, in 105, they were turned into a programme of extraordinary games, that is to say games not scheduled in the traditional programme. Gradually it became the custom for magistrates to offer them as a gesture of thanks, when they took office in Rome or in other Roman cities. These bloody spectacles, on which the ancients were extremely keen, were not linked to a sacrifice or a cult.

5 *LECTISTERNIA*, *SELLISTERNIA*, SUPPLICATIONS, EXPIATIONS

From 399 BC on, the Romans from time to time celebrated *lectisternia* and *sellisternia*. These were great sacrifical banquets at which several deities (six or twelve) were installed on dining couches or chairs in some consecrated place. Goddesses, like Roman *matronae*, took part seated on chairs (*sellisternia*). Introduced on the recommendation of a Sibylline oracle, the *lectisternium* was originally a ritual designed to restore concord between the gods and the Romans. A kind of *lectisternium* had already figured among earlier, strictly Roman traditions. On the occasion of a birth, a couch and a table would be set up in the atrium of a leading family's house, in honour of Juno Lucina and Hercules; and a couch would also be available for Pilumnus and Picumnus, two divine protectors of mothers who had just given birth. The Sibylline oracle of 399 was inspired by the Greek tradition of banquets shared between men and gods (theoxeny), to create a Roman ritual adapted to its new context. Little by little, this ritual of reconciliation spread, until eventually most cult sites and festivals organised their own *lectisternia*. This picturesque ceremony now offered a variant or complement to the traditional sacrificial banquet.

Supplication appears to have been a truly ancient ritual. Wearing wreaths and carrying branches of laurel, Roman men would do the rounds of cult sites, accompanied by their wives and children, to 'supplicate' the gods. They prostrated themselves to beg for help in times of danger or to thank them in times of victory and success. Incense and wine would be offered to the gods, and *matronae* would kneel on the ground and sweep it with their hair. Under the Empire, supplication with incense and wine was a ritual particularly associated with ceremonies connected to the imperial house. Supplication dramatised the ritual of *praefatio*, the solemn salutation of the gods, and extended it to all the Roman deities in a spectacular and 'realistic' manner. At root, a supplication was a particularly solemn *praefatio* celebrated by all citizens.

Under the Republic, *lectisternia* and supplications, often celebrated in conjunction, were frequently associated with processions that led choirs of girls from the sanctuary of Apollo (*in Circo*) right round to the Capitol and Palatine. Under the Empire, this type of ceremony was replaced by the Secular Games and the centenary festivals of Rome. The Secular Games, whose history in the Republican period remains obscure, were celebrated on the recommendation of a Sibylline oracle, to bring to an end a period of one hundred and ten years, the maximum duration of a 'generation' (*saeculum*), and to request success and wellbeing for the next *saeculum*. Under the Empire, the gods honoured were the Moirai, Ilithyia and the Terra Mater on the one hand, and Jupiter, Juno, Apollo and Diana on the other. The festival proper lasted three whole days, during which sacrifices were celebrated both by night and by day in a number of places (the Campus Martius, the Capitol, the Palatine). It ended with a procession of boys and girls singing a 'secular' hymn several times in succession. An extra week of theatrical and circus games followed on after the rites. Celebrated for the fifth time (so it was said) under Augustus in 17 BC, these games were repeated in AD 88 by Domitian and in 204 by Septimius Severus. To make the most of the pomp and ceremony of the Secular Games, from the reign of Claudius on (AD 48), Roman rulers also celebrated the centenaries of the foundation of Rome, using a very similar set of rituals. After the celebration of the ninth centenary in 148, Rome's millennium was commemorated in 248, under Philip the Arab.

Chapter 7
Auspices and rituals of divination

1 GENERAL PRINCIPLES

We know virtually nothing about divination in the archaic period and even relatively ancient documents such as the inauguration formula for the *templum* on the *arx* on the Capitoline hill (Varro, *On the Latin Language*, 7.8) have come down to us cast in later language. On the other hand, the last two centuries of the Republic is a period marvellously well documented for any study of Roman divination. There is plenty of direct evidence and, furthermore, Cicero's treatise *On Divination* provides us with a selection of learned opinions on divinatory practices, both for and against. During this period public divination depended on auspices, Sibylline oracles, extispicy (the reading of entrails) and haruspicy, and occasionally involved the consultation of foreign oracles. Private divination was more eclectic, for side by side with traditional auspices people turned to astrologers and itinerant soothsayers. Under the Empire, practices evolved. General institutional changes were reflected in the field of public divination: auspices and the consultation of Sibylline oracles no longer played a primary role, while the interpretation of prodigies and the techniques of astrological prognosis gained in importance. Meanwhile at the private level the unification of the Empire and the extension of the Roman people favoured the spread of techniques of divination from every corner of the Empire.

It is the divinatory system of the first century BC that is the best known to us and the most fully attested. So let us concentrate on this period, for it will allow us to make a detailed analysis of mechanisms of divination and the spirit in which it was conducted. There is virtually no mention of any revolution in attitudes or practice either before or after this period; so it is fair to assume that by and large they remained unchanged down to the third century AD.

In the first century BC, the Roman system of divination as a whole was ruled by one principle, which Cicero observes and comments upon in his dialogue *On Divination*. Divinatory consultation was considered to be an almost automatic technique. Even the defender of the 'credulous' position in Cicero's dialogue does not dispute that fact, for he attributes to divine will the ability to change the natural order to announce whatever it pleases. Divination was a deliberate and precise human technique which consisted not so much in an empirical and direct consultation with the gods, but rather in the recitation of a kind of prayer that revealed the gods' agreement with whoever was consulting them. In a way, that consultation with the gods was comparable to a magistrate's consultations with the people. It referred to specific questions; it generally produced either yes or no for an answer; and it was organised under the control of the magistrates. It was a matter of rituals that followed the traditional rules absolutely exactly and left no room at all for sentiment. It therefore makes no sense to denounce Roman divination, as some scholars have, as an indication of the decadence of true religious feeling in Rome: the traditions of divination completely conformed to the ritualistic principles of Roman piety.

2 THE AUSPICES

The task of taking the auspices fell to the magistrates and was an essential requirement before any public action was initiated. As the name indicates (*auspicium*, from **aui-spicium*, 'the observation of birds'), the magistrates' observations were limited to the signs conveyed by birds. Augurs, in contrast, 'augured' or 'inaugurated', but did not take auspices. They had the right to announce 'oblative' auguries (see below) noticed by themselves or others. In view of the complexity of the formal divinatory system, the augurs served as the advisors to magistrates on any problems relating to auspices which they might face. However, at all levels, the magistrates always retained supreme authority over the process of divination. It was up to them to accept and establish the significance of all signs noticed and announced and also to decide whether or not to consult Sibylline or foreign oracles.

There were two types of auspices: auspices and auguries (signs) *requested* from the gods (*auspicia/auguria impetratiua*) and auguries not requested but that *declared themselves* of their own accord – or, rather, as the gods willed (*auspicia/ auguria oblatiua*). These could be any phenomena that seemed significant or unusual: they ranged from ambiguous remarks that came to the notice of the magistrate or his entourage, stumbles and falls, or hitches that occurred in the course of a ceremony, to surprising natural phenomena and natural catastrophes. If it was sufficiently serious, such a sign would rank as a prodigy. One difference was that an oblative augury could either be accepted or rejected by the magistrate in question, while a prodigy was generally accepted without question and expiated forthwith (see below).

2.1 *Auspicia impetratiua*

'Impetrative' auspices were taken in accordance with a set of rules fixed in advance and reserved exclusively for public activities such as the investiture of magistrates or the important decisions that they had to take (calling assemblies, departures overseas, battles and so on). In order to take the auspices, the magistrate first pitched a tent on a particular spot. This was the *auguraculum*, which would previously have been defined and 'inaugurated' by the augurs. Auspices could only be requested from an *auguraculum*. In Rome, there were three of these: on the citadel (the *Arx*), on the Quirinal and on the Palatine. Auspices did not produce advice on action or foretell the future, and they never revealed the causes for events in the past. They were concerned exclusively with divine approval or dispproval for a particular future public action. The auspices were always taken before *comitia* were convoked, that is to say a magistrate always consulted the sovereign god Jupiter before any important public decision was reached.

Since Roman space was divided up into very precise categories, a magistrate had to renew the auspices (that is to say consult heaven as to the legitimacy of his decision and his power) every time he crossed one of its boundaries, often a stream or a river. In Rome, the *amnis Petronia* constituted one of these boundaries; it was a stream that separated the *urbs* (city) from the Campus Martius – that is to say that separated the Senate and the Forum from the place where the centuriate assembly met. If a magistrate wished to consult the Senate while these *comitia* were assembled in the Campus Martius, he had to return to the 'city' and then take the auspices again when he was back in the Campus Martius. A magistrate also had to take the auspices before entering upon his duties and before leaving Rome on a mission outside it. When on a military campaign, a magistrate would set up an *auguraculum* in his camp for day-to-day auspices, but the auspices for an investiture were in principle to be requested only in Rome itself.

Auguries and auspices

The inauguration of King Numa: the model for investiture auspices

He (Numa) commanded that, just as Romulus had obeyed the augural omens in building his city and assuming regal power, so too in his own case the gods should be consulted. Accordingly an augur (who thereafter, as a mark of honour, was made a priest of the state in permanent charge of that function) conducted him to the citadel (the *Arx*, to the east of the Capitol) and caused him to sit down on a stone facing the south. The augur seated himself on Numa's left, having his head covered and holding in his right hand the crooked staff without a knot, which they call a *lituus*. Then, looking out over the city and the country beyond, he prayed to the gods, and marked off the heavens by a line from east to west, designating as 'right' the regions to the south, as 'left' those to the north, and fixing in his ▶

▶ mind a landmark opposite to him and as far away as the eye could reach; next shifting the crook to his left hand and laying his right hand on Numa's head, he uttered the following prayer: 'Father Jupiter, if it is Heaven's will that this man Numa Pompilius, whose head I am touching, be king in Rome, do thou exhibit to us unmistakable signs within those limits which I have set.' He then specified the auspices which he desired should be sent, and upon their appearance Numa was declared king.

Livy, *History of Rome*, 1.18.6–10

Taking the auspices at the end of the Republic

Granting that there are auspices (as there are not), certainly those which we ordinarily employ – whether by the *tripudium* or by observation of the heavens – are not auspices in any sense, but are the mere ghosts of auspices.

'*Quintus Fabius, I wish you to assist me at the auspices.*' He answers, '*I will.*' (In our forefathers' time the magistrates on such occasions used to call in some expert person to take the auspices – but in these days anyone will do. But one must be an expert to know what constitutes 'silence', for by that term we mean 'free of every augural defect". To understand that belongs to a perfect augur). After the celebrant has said to his assistant, '*Tell me when silence appears to exist*', the latter, without looking up or about him, immediately replies, '*Silence appears to exist.*' Then the celebrant says, '*Tell me when the chickens begin to eat.*' '*They are eating now*', is the answer. But what are these birds they are talking about, and where are they? Someone replies, 'It's poultry. It's in a cage and the person who brought it is called "a poulterer" because of his business.' These, then, are the messengers of Jove! What difference does it make whether they eat or not? None, so far as the auspices are concerned. But because of the fact that, while they eat, some food must necessarily fall from their mouths and strike upon the ground (*terram pavire*) – this at first was called *terripavium*, and later, *terripudium*; now it is called *tripudium* – therefore when a crumb of food falls from a chicken's mouth a *tripudium solistimum* [a perfect *tripudium*] is announced to the celebrant.

Cicero, *On Divination*, 2.34.71–2 (standard formulae for a consultation given in italics)

But let us return to what happened at the tent set up by the 'auspicant'. He rested in the tent until the moment for taking the auspices, just before dawn. The auspices were valid only for the one day and only for the particular decision to be taken. They concerned the legitimacy of the magistrate and his decision, as it were within a given space: if he left the *pomerium* or whatever the limit was, the auspices were no longer valid. In the historical period, the consultation itself consisted in an exchange of questions and answers between the auspicant and his assistant. The assistant was not an augur but one of the magistrate's attendants (his chicken-keeper, *pullarius*). In ancient times, the auspices were taken by observing the flight of birds. But from the third century BC at least Roman magistrates preferred to 'observe' chickens; the taking of the auspices was supposed to involve the observation of these birds' appetite and general behaviour. In the historical period, any Roman magistrate on the move would have among his entourage cages full of chickens that were looked after by a chicken-keeper. In theory, the fact that the chickens were eating, were eating greedily, or were eating sparingly or not at all produced, respectively, a favourable answer, a very favourable answer or a negative one. However, if we are to believe Cicero and the evidence of Roman historians, the answer was in effect always positive; that is, it always indicated what the magistrate wanted. In fact, the whole scenario constituted the necessary framework for a ritual announcement that the auspices were favourable, rather than a procedure of divinatory inquiry. The magistrate really used this rite to announce his own firm conviction that his decision met with the approval of the gods.

2.2 Auspicia oblativa *and prodigies*

Every day many surprising incidents of all kinds occurred. The chances were that every magistrate would witness some such event; and his entourage and the public generally kept a lookout for disturbing incidents and, if necessary, announced them. The ancients thought that all these signs possessed either a favourable or an unfavourable meaning either for the Republic or for an individual. The more enlightened elite, however, recommended not attributing everything to the will of the gods and not living in anxiety about every small sign. According to this view, the whole skill of a pious man lay in recognising the dividing line between a calm resolve based on trust in the benevolence of the gods and an obstinate refusal to recognise 'real' signs. In the last analysis, it was above all success or failure that defined the divinatory skill of a magistrate or an individual – and divine benevolence.

Certain signs, usually *oblativa*, were clearly in a different league from auspices: these were prodigies. Unlike auspices, prodigies were believed to announce some important event that was either fortunate or unfortunate. Like *auspicia oblativa*, prodigies only existed once a magistrate (or an individual) had recognised them to be such. Frequently a prodigy consisted in some disaster that punished the Roman people: a natural catastrophe, an epidemic, a defeat – all could be seen as manifestations of divine wrath. A prodigy expressed the 'true' nature of the deity directly, at the cost of devastating effects, in order to indicate that the gods' interests had been injured by the Romans. The Roman pontiffs collected together all reports of prodigies that had occurred in the course of the year, both in Rome and in other Roman cities, so as to examine their meaning and expiate them in Rome or, as the case might be, elsewhere in Italy. The signs that seemed most important or dangerous were examined by the Senate at the New Year and were expiated on its orders. Particularly alarming prodigies were passed on immediately from the pontiffs to the magistrates and the Senate. Generally, a prodigy signified some omission or error committed in cult, and the pontiffs were ordered first to offer an expiatory sacrifice in order to conciliate the injured deity, then to repeat the rite whose procedures had been incorrect or had some element omitted, and in some instances also to make reparation for the damages suffered by the property of the gods.

2.3 Auspices and legitimacy

According to public law, auspices were one of the formal elements necessary for any decision to be legitimate. For that reason, they were often attacked or contested by political opponents. A magistrate of equal or higher rank could challenge the legitimacy of the auspices by announcing an unfavourable 'oblative' sign (usually a clap of thunder) or by denouncing some formal mistake in the ritual. Challenging auspices was formalised to the point where the challenger had only to announce by an edict that 'he would be observing' on the day when his colleague intended to take action to signify that an unfavourable augury had by chance been obtained. But in most cases, the authority of the magistrate taking action carried the day, for his will counted for even more than the sign itself: even if he realised that the sign announced as favourable was not in fact so (suppose, for example, the chicken-keeper had not taken into account some abnormal behaviour on the part of his chickens that crossed the line separating what was normal from a prodigy), he could nevertheless decide that he had received a favourable augury from his assistant and that he was accepting it as such. What mattered above all was not the sign but the decision of the magistrate taking the auspices. The only way to challenge the auspices of a magistrate of the highest rank was to refer the matter to the college of augurs and the Senate and denounce some technical mistake. Such a protest could only be made by a man who held *imperium*, and could not apply to military auspices. Only augurs possessed the right to postpone *comitia* by announcing that they were 'adjourned' (*alio die*), thereby implying that the augurs had observed an unfavourable sign (such as, for example, lightning or a thunderclap) in the course of the *comitia* in question. Even so, their announcement was only valid for that one day.

Under the Republic, the auspices constituted one of the foundations of public liberty. On the one hand, they guaranteed the magistrates' freedom of action; on the other, they imposed upon them so many rules and limitations that they could act only if they took a thousand and one precautions, for there was always the possibility of a challenge and subsequent annulment of a public action. Once the legitimacy of the ritual was established, so too was that of the decision and its effects, for it was accepted that the sovereign god had given his approval. At the end of the Republic, in the course of the conflicts that divided the various factions struggling for supremacy, the auspices were the focus of intense controversy. It was now as much a matter of denouncing the illegitimacy of your opponents and proclaiming legitimacy conferred on yourself as of emphasising that you were yourself the only person qualified to actualise the support that the gods offered the Romans. In just half a century, the auspices had been transformed from a guarantee of public liberty into a component of personal power.

2.4 The evolution of the auspices after the civil wars

After the struggle between Caesar and Pompey, Augustus transformed the system of auspices, giving it a new political orientation. By repeatedly occupying the consulate, along with his friends, during the decade following the victory of Actium (31 BC), he took possession *de facto* of the urban auspices. And when, in 27 BC, the Senate charged him with the task of administering the 'armed' provinces, thereby in effect commanding all the legions (bar one, which was under the power of the proconsul of Africa), he alone controlled the *imperium* and the *auspicia militiae*. Once he was the sole legitimate commander of the armies, Augustus lost no time in restricting the right of a triumph to himself and fellow members of the imperial house who held an exceptional degree of *imperium*; for, to be able to celebrate a triumph, it was necessary to have possessed the auspices throughout the war in question. From now on, wars were under the leadership (*ductu*) of a general, but under the auspices of the emperor.

Augustus breathed new life into the archaic tradition of the auspices taken from the flight of birds (he is said to have spotted twelve vultures on the occasion of his investiture as a consul in 43 BC: see Suetonius, *Life of the Deified Augustus*, 95); but actually he profoundly transformed the whole system. The auspices did not disappear under the Empire. Roman magistrates continued to be flanked by a chicken-keeper and his chickens, and the formula mentioned above, according to which wars took place 'under the auspices of the emperor', was no empty collection of words. However, given that the Augustan system was designed to eliminate the risk of clashes between the various holders of *imperium*, conflicts over legitimacy granted by the auspices no longer occurred. And since those quarrels were by and large the reason why historians mentioned the auspices at all, our information about them has disappeared along with the conflicts.

Magistrates did continue to take the auspices, but in a new context. The system underwent the same evolution as the popular assemblies. Like these, the auspices continued to be indispensable from a legal point of view for important public decisions and for conferring power on magistrates, but to the extent that real power now rested higher up, progressively they became purely formal rules. In effect, the purpose of the auspices shifted towards the affirmation of the emperor's legitimacy or illegitimacy. We know at least one occasion when the auspices were taken on the proclamation of an emperor (Suetonius, *Life of Nero*, 8). And other sources give a story (inevitably biased) of the signs that heralded an individual's imminent elevation to the purple, or an emperor's fall from power. From the point of view of ritual, the system seems to have remained intact, but its political use changed.

The auspices also existed in the colonies and the *municipia*. So much is indicated by the existence of municipal augurs, as well as some other isolated pieces of evidence. Inscribed *cippi* (marker stones) discovered at Banzi (Bantia) initially raised great hopes, as they seemed to be related to the *auguraculum* of a Roman colony. But further detailed research did not confirm that impression, so these *cippi* remain mysterious. As for private auspices, all that have survived in our sources are a few references to nuptial auspices.

3 THE SIBYLLINE BOOKS

When prodigies occurred again and again, and the Roman authorities were unable to assuage the anger of the gods by ordinary rites of procuration, they consulted the Sibylline oracle to discover the cause of their problems and the solution to them.

3.1 The history of the Sibylline Books

At the end of the Republic, there were three Sibylline Books. They contained prophecies, written in Greek hexameters, which a Sibyl from Cumae was said to have sold to King Tarquin. At first they were kept in the undercroft of the temple of Capitoline Jupiter, the master of signs, but in 18 BC Augustus transferred them to the temple of Apollo Palatine. In 83 BC, the books had been destroyed by a fire on the Capitol. A senatorial committee tried to replace the collection using documents found in the Italian colonies and in cities that boasted a Sibyl (in particular Erythraea, in Ionia). It brought back to Rome a thousand or so lines of Sibylline poetry, and these sufficed to reconstitute the archive. It was examined and expurgated by both Augustus and Tiberius. The Romans do not seem to have been much bothered about the actual content of the books. They did not lament the destruction of the three Capitoline books as an irreplaceable loss, but were quite happy to reconstruct them. All that preoccupied them was that the collection should be reconstituted and preserved. All the lines of poetry approved by the College of the *(quin)decemuiri* and the Senate were now known as the Sibylline Books. The thousand lines of poetry collected by the committee of 83 BC thus continued to be used throughout the imperial period. The (new) Books were considered to be a talisman for Rome, and their destruction by Stilicho in the early fifth century provoked a riot in Rome.

3.2 Consulting the Sibylline Books

The books were consulted when particularly alarming prodigies were noticed – prodigies that gave warning of and often themselves stood for a breakdown in the relations between the gods and the Romans. The books were believed to contain explanations for prodigies and the steps to be taken in order to put things right. Consultations were concerned only with the interests of the state.

On the surface, the Sibylline oracles were quite different from auspices in that they represented the words of a Sibyl directly inspired by a god. But in fact the principles of divination underlying them were very close to those of the auspices. In the first place, the prophecies were a closed, limited and fixed collection. Second, the very procedure of consultation showed its extremely Roman character. The books were consulted upon the orders of a magistrate and the Senate. The consultation was carried out by the *(quin)decemuiri*, who were responsible for consulting the Sibylline Books behind closed doors. Two oracles of 125 BC, carefully preserved, and two written accounts, one in Cicero (*On Divination*, 2.110), the other in Dionysius of Halicarnassus (4.62.6) give us some idea of the procedure. The priests seem to have selected one or two lines from the books, by means that escape us (by lot? on the basis of significant words?). They wrote these at the top of what was to be the oracle and from them built up an acrostic in which the individual letters of the first line/s, in order, formed the first letters of the lines that followed. With the aid of assistants with a knowledge of Greek, the priests then filled in the various lines of the acrostic in hexameter verse, and these conveyed the Sibylline oracle. These hexameters invariably prescribed rituals that were very Roman in character: processions, offerings, sacrifices (some of which would be celebrated according to the 'Greek rite'), *lectisternia* and Games. Sometimes they also recommended inviting a new deity or cult to Rome and installing it there. The best-known example of this is the Great Mother.

We do not know whether all oracles were composed in this fashion. The very brief recommendations that the sources mention could in fact come from longer oracles or from a 'real' Sibylline line. But at any rate, once the oracle was

composed, the priests passed it on to the Senate, which then
decided with the consulting magistrate what measures should
be adopted and how they should be applied. The result of the
consultation was announced and dictated to the people in the
form of an edict. The cults established by the oracles continued in many cases to be supervised by the college of
(quin)decemuiri: the election of priests of the Great Mother,
for example, in the Roman colonies required the formal
approval of the *(quin)decemviri*, as is attested well into the
third century AD.

4 THE *HARUSPICES* AND READING THE *EXTA*

In the course of every sacrifice, those officiating proceeded to
an act of divination by examining the state of the *exta*
(entrails). Modern historians call this 'extispicy', the inspection of the *exta*. If the five elements that made up the entrails
showed no anomalies, the sacrifice was accepted. If not, the
sacrifice had to be repeated. The acceptance of the sacrifice
was called the *litatio*.

In the course of that inspection, the celebrant of the
sacrifice was aided by an assistant called a *haruspex*. This
type of official was to be found in the entourages of all Roman
magistrates and authorities and likewise, in the colonies, in
the entourages of the *duouiri*. They should not be confused
with the great Etruscan *haruspices* of the Republican period,
or with the *haruspices* who 'worked privately'. Under the
Empire, the *haruspices* working with magistrates and pro-
magistrates were grouped in an *ordo* of sixty *haruspices*.

That same operation of examining the *exta* sometimes gave
rise to a different type of divination, which was traced back to
the Etruscans. The state of the various organs that made up
the entrails could be analysed in detail with a view to produ-
cing a prognosis. This technique was called haruspicy and, in
all likelihood, it was carried out by the same practitioners.
Genuinely Etruscan haruspicy went far beyond an examination of the *exta*. Its purpose was to explain prodigies of every

kind. From the Punic Wars onward, the Roman Senate regularly turned to the Etruscan *haruspices*. They were descended from the great aristocratic families of Etruria and possessed ancestral knowledge that they applied to the Roman context. From their analyses of prodigies, they produced either explanations very similar to those of augurs or *(quin)decemuiri*, or predictions. They would predict victories or defeats, or they might decide that a prodigy indicated the illegitimacy of some magistrate. In any event, the Roman authorities used their replies in the same way as those given by the auspices and the Sibylline Books.

Recourse to foreign oracles was not prohibited, although in the second century BC the Senate did remonstrate with certain consuls because they had consulted the oracle of Praeneste, which counted as foreign. In exactly the same way, the father of the Gracchi had challenged a response of the *haruspices* that was unfavourable to him, underlining the fact that they were foreign. Nevertheless, consultations with Italic oracles and even the Delphic oracle were quite common. They complemented and enriched the practices of divination at Rome and, in the case of Delphi, also lent international authority to the recommendations obtained. After the Roman conquest of the world, most of the great oracles of Italy (such as Praeneste) and the Mediterranean (Delphi, for example) lost their renown and their power. But from the second century AD on, once the conquered countries had been integrated into the Roman Empire, the great international oracles such as those at Claros and Didyma gained a second lease of life.

5 PRIVATE DIVINATION

Just as magistrates and the Senate did, individuals resorted constantly to diviners. We have already come across nuptial auspices. In private sacrifices too, the celebrants used *extispicium* and probably also *haruspicina*. We know from a number of documents that great families and modest ones alike consulted *haruspices*, Chaldaean astrologers (*mathematici*) and other prophets of a variety of origins in order to obtain explanations for prodigies and also protection from them. So, for example, the father of the Gracchi, who complained so bitterly to the Senate about the Etruscan *haruspices*, nevertheless himself consulted *haruspices* about a prodigy noted in his own household, and furthermore accepted their interpretation. Two and a half centuries later, Pliny the Younger was advised by *haruspices* to rebuild a sanctuary of Ceres situated on his land.

We know hardly anything about the private *haruspices*. Were they established or itinerant? Roman or Etruscan? Were they the very same as those consulted by the magistrates and the *duouiri*? There were probably many different kinds of diviners. Those who advised senatorial families were probably not the ones who offered their services in the streets of Rome or out in the countryside. But whatever the case may be, such evidence as exists suggests that divination also played an important role in private life, although we do not know what type of divination was most popular: the kind that proclaimed that relations with the gods were good or the kind that tried to penetrate the unknown.

At any rate, private divination could be practised more intensely and could use forbidden means to acquire greater knowledge and foresee the future. Such techniques resorted to the same methods as devotions and enchantments. The 'sorceror' had to insinuate himself into intimacy with the gods so as to obtain the coveted information. These rites, which, at least as imagined by the Romans, were associated with the violation of tombs and even human sacrifices, had a bad reputation.

Astrology, which had spread in Rome hand in hand with Hellenism, became progressively one of the most important techniques of private divination. Under the Empire, it was just as common as haruspicy, at every level of society. Like magical divination, the casting of horoscopes was considered a violent religious technique, for it made it possible to know the fate of your enemy. Accusations of treason often included a charge of having resorted to astrological consultation in order to discover the date of the emperor's death. Hardly surprisingly, astrologers and other prophets were regularly rounded up and expelled from Rome on account of the scandals that their practices caused.

Part IV
The Actors

Chapter 8
Priestly figures

1 WHO WERE THE PRIESTS IN ROME?

The term *sacerdos* (**sakro-dho-ts*, 'the one who does the sacred act') should not give the impression that there was a caste of priests in Roman public and private religion. The term is sometimes used as a title (for example, for the *sacerdos publica Cereris*), sometimes to designate priests generally, of whatever kind; but it does not cover all the agents of religion. If, by priests we understand all those who celebrated religious rituals, then *sacerdos* certainly does not cover them all. In fact, every citizen was a priest in as much as that, as the father of a family, he presided over the cult of his domestic community. Furthermore, all those who held authority in public life, at whatever level – magistrate, promagistrate, legate, centurion, college president, or president of a local district, and so on – were also responsible for the cult of the community that they led. Most sacrifices and festivals were celebrated by these men, not by priests in the strict sense of the term. Even senators and, in the colonies and *municipia*, the decurions collectively fulfilled functions which, from a modern point of view, seem eminently priestly. Every important decision involving religion, every innovation and disagreement relating to a religious problem that affected the public cult or other cults that were celebrated in public, fell within their domain. In certain cases it was, by law, the people itself, as a whole, that officiated collectively or took religious decisions.

None of these religous agents had been consecrated or 'called'. They were simply invested with these priestly functions by virtue of their social role or because they had been elected. It is true that in the Roman world there was no difference between 'secular' life and religious life. Every public act was religious and every religious act was public; sacred law was simply an offshoot of ordinary public law. In consequence, a magistrate was invested (in some cases actually by the auspices) with a function that extended to two complementary fields of action, namely relations with the gods and relations with men. And that applied to all holders of authority as well as to magistrates themselves. What is more, ritual actions performed by magistrates or other community leaders were no different from those made by priests. A sacrifice was a sacrifice whether it was offered by a pontiff or by the president of a town district (*uicomagister*). The only differences lay in the particular cult concerned – the ritual in each cult being, in effect, reserved for those who found themselves charged with performing it. No priest, for example, could celebrate the ritual of a triumph or of the presidency of the Roman or the Plebeian Games just on the strength of his being a priest; and no holder of authority could, simply on that basis, celebrate the rites of inauguration or a sacrifice to Dea Dia. However, it should be added that priestly functions were virtually all compatible with other public functions, so you might say that the Romans were regularly switching from one role to another. Sometimes a magistrate or a senator would act as such, and sometimes he would exercise a priestly role, but he could never confuse the two roles. He was either the one *or* the other, never both at once. Even the emperor could not act simultaneously as both *princeps* and *pontifex maximus* (chief pontiff).

Those who were called priests were not, in any case, 'men of god' or people devoted entirely to the service of the deity. Some priests might be subjected to extremely exacting ritual obligations (the *flamen* of Jupiter and his wife and, for example, the Vestals), but those are isolated examples and – in the case of the Vestals – temporary. As a general rule, a priest was a citizen like any other. He was elected by his peers (*cooptatio*) or by the people, and never received any prior training. His duties were limited to specific actions and did not extend to general religious competence. No priest, not even the *pontifex maximus*, was responsible in all areas. Private cults were entirely separate from the power of the public priests; the priests were, in any case, far too restricted in numbers to control anything other than the great public acts of the Roman State. Despite what one modern myth would have us believe, there were no religious or priestly books containing a full account of doctrine and liturgies. The books of the colleges of priests were annual reports in which ritual procedures, celebrations and decisions were registered as and when they took place. They were called 'commentaries'. These documents, some of them ancient, were a mine of information for antiquarians and historians, who extracted from them many items of information which they then set out in their own treatises; it was these which their contemporaries gradually took to calling *libri sacerdotum, pontificum,* etc., so helping to create a myth of 'the priestly books' that has proved extremely tenacious.

The majority of priests and celebrants were male, free and Roman citizens. A slave could never officiate in his own name but could do so in that of his master. Women were not excluded from active religious life, except in certain cults (Silvanus and Hercules), but they could not take on any representative religious function on behalf of the state. They could officiate for themselves or for other women, but not for the Roman people or for the family as a whole. Even within the family, they could not cut up the meat or prepare the ritual flour: that role fell to men. Although they were passive in most public cults and did not take part in communal sacrificial banquets, they did attend Games and took the leading role in the cults of *matronae* – for example, in the cults of Bona Dea, Pudicitia, Fortuna Muliebris and Juno Caprotina. In the Secular Games, matrons celebrated a public *sellisternium* in honour of Juno and Diana, which implied a sacrifice, but they did so only when the public sacrifices offered by men were over. At supplications, they were at their husbands' sides, as they were also in domestic rites. Finally, there was nothing to prevent a woman or a girl from acting as an assistant during a ritual. In short, the ritual roles of women varied according to the context, and it is incorrect simply to declare that Roman women were excluded from religion.

2 THE PUBLIC PRIESTS OF ROME

In the historical period the public priests of Rome – whose exact title was *sacerdos*, pontiff or whatever 'of the Roman people, and the Quirites' – fell into two groups: either what were known as the major colleges, or the sodalities. There were also a number of priests of particular deities, and priests of the ancient Latin communities. The most important public priests of Rome held their position for life and benefited from immunity to public charges and taxes. They also enjoyed the privilege of banqueting at the expense of the people and could occupy places of honour at the Games. They had the right to make announcements to the people by issuing edicts, and to be questioned by the Senate. They may also have had the right to convoke ordinary meetings of the people (*contio*), but not *comitia*.

In public life, in particular when officiating, priests wore the *toga praetexta*, and some also had other special costumes. Augurs wore a purple *trabea*, and male priests wore a kind of cap (a *galerus*). It is known that the *flamen* of Jupiter wore a *galerus* made from the skin of a sacrificial victim topped with an olive branch (*apex*), and his toga was made of wool (*laena*). A *flamen*'s wife wore her hair in a *tutulus*. The Vestals wore the dress of a Roman *matrona* and a bride's veil, and also had a special way of styling their hair.

2.1 The major colleges

Up until 196 BC there were three major colleges: first, in hierarchical order, the pontiffs; next the augurs; then the *decemuiri*. In 196, a fourth college was formally created, the *tresuiri epulonum*. The membership of these colleges steadily increased in number up until the Augustan period.

The pontiffs, who were under the authority of the *pontifex maximus*, advised the magistrates, the Senate and the other priestly colleges on the rites and customs of the traditional religion and on sacred law. They provided advice to individuals on possible conflict between private rituals and public sacred law. They are believed to have played a central role in the development of the most ancient civil law, which they supervised up until 304 BC. Amongst other things, they had a powerful influence on legal business thanks to their control of the calendar. We know that the *Lex Ogulnia* (300 BC) ruled that there should be nine pontiffs; then Sulla's priestly law (82) increased the number to fifteen; under Caesar (46) it was fixed at sixteen. In 300 BC five of the pontiffs were patricians, four plebeians; previously all had been patrician. In addition to the pontiffs themselves, the college included the *rex sacrorum* (king of the sacred rites) who, together with his wife (the *regina sacrorum*), celebrated a number of rituals believed to date right back to the kings of Rome; fifteen *flamines*, three of whom were known as 'major' (because they were patricians) and twelve minor, three minor pontiffs and, finally, the six Vestal Virgins, who guarded and tended the public hearth. Under the Empire, the *flamines* of Caesar, Augustus and other deified emperors also appear to have been members of the college of pontiffs. Unlike the pontiffs, whose main task was to supervise the rules governing public cult, the job of the *flamines* was to celebrate rituals. The best-known of them, the *flamen* of Jupiter, represented the function of Jupiter (and was, in a sense, the god's 'double') through the obligations and prohibitions to which he was subject. The insignia or emblems of the pontiffs, which appeared on coins and monuments, were a ladle, a jug, a knife and a *galerus* (cap).

The public priests of Rome under the Republic
The major colleges

The college of pontiffs	Pontiffs (3, 5, from the *Lex Ogulnia* on 9, from Sulla on 15, from Caesar on 16, then probably 19 from Augustus on). *Rex sacrorum* (king of the sacred rites) plus *regina sacrorum*. 3 major *flamines* (of Jupiter, Mars and Quirinus). 12 minor *flamines* (*Carmentalis, Cerialis, Falacer, Floralis, Furrinalis, Palatualis, Pomonalis, Portunalis, Volcanalis, Volturnalis* and two others unknown). Major *flamines* and *rex sacrorum* = patrician. Pontiffs originally patrician; in 300, 5 patrician plus 4 plebeian. 6 Vestal Virgins (president: *Virgo Vestalis Maxima*); (later) *flamines* of deified emperors. President: *pontifex maximus*.	The pontiffs advised on religious traditions and sacred law, when asked to do so by magistrates, priests or the Senate. They controlled the *sacra*, sacred places and cemeteries. They established the calendar and organised its intercalation. The *flamines* celebrated the cult and established the presence of the god whose name they bore. The Vestals tended the public hearth.
The college of augurs	3, 6, from the *Lex Ogulnia* on 9, from Sulla on 15, from Caesar on 16, then, probably from Augustus on, 19. Originally patrician; in 300, 5 patrician, 4 plebeian. President: the oldest of them.	Controlled the auspices, assisted magistrates (signs), inaugurations.
The college of the *(quin) decemuiri*, responsible for consulting the Sibylline Books	2, from 367 BC on 10, from the second century BC on 15, from Caesar on 19. Originally patrician; in 367, 5 patrician, 5 plebeian. President: one or several yearly *magistri*.	Looked after and consulted the Sibylline Books, verified the application of Sibylline oracles.
The college of the *septemuiri*	In 196 BC 3, from the *Lex Domitia* on 7, from Augustus on 10, possibly a few more.	Controlled the Roman Games, and probably also all the other public Games.

▶

▶ **The sodalities**

Fetiales	20(?), operated in pairs (the *uerbenarius* and the *pater patratus*).	Ritually communicated the diplomatic decisions of the Senate (war, treaties, ultimata).
The salii	2 companies of 12 members each: the *salii* of the Palatine and of the Quirinal. Patrician. Their function was incompatible with a magistracy or any other priesthood. President: the *praesul*.	Linked with Mars; processions and dances in the streets of Rome.
The luperci	2 groups, the *luperci Quinctiales* and the *luperci Fabiani*. Under Caesar, temporarily, also the *luperci Iuliani*. 12 members in each group(?).	Celebrated the Lupercalia (15 February).
The Arval Brethren	12. President: the annual *magister*, assisted by a *flamen*.	Celebrated the sacrifice to Dea Dia (late May).

Special priesthoods

Curiones	30, elected by the *comitia curiata*. From 209 BC all plebeians. President: the *curio maximus*.	Celebrated the sacrifices of the *curiae*
The public priestess of Ceres	In theory a native of Magna Graecia; of low social status.	Celebrated the rituals of *matronae* introduced into the cult of Ceres at the end of the third century.
The high priest(ess) of the Great Mother	In theory, non-Roman; of low social status.	Together with the *galli* (president: the *archigallus*), celebrated the Phrygian rites of the Great Mother.

The augures, whose numbers increased in step with those of the pontiffs, were responsible for auspical law, for inaugurations and various ways of defining space. They also celebrated occasional rituals of divination, such as the *augurium salutis*, which took place in periods of total peace and was related to success for the Roman people in the coming year. We also know that they offered up sacrifices on the *Arx*, according to secret formulae (this does not mean that all the formulae that they used were secret). Thanks to Varro, we know the formula used for the creation of a *templum* on the ground, probably that of the *auguraculum* on the *Arx*. Also according to Varro, the formulae would vary depending on the context. The emblem of augurs was a small 'crook', the *lituus*, which they held while they officiated at rituals.

Up until the time of Sulla, there were ten guardians of the Sibylline Books (the *decemuiri*). The *Lex Cornelia* increased these to fifteen (*quindecemuiri*), and under Caesar or Augustus, their number increased to nineteen. They took care of the books, consulted them, and sometimes supervised how the oracles were acted upon. A number of public rituals, whether or not recommended by the Sibylline oracle, were also entrusted to them. Their emblem was a tripod.

The *tresuiri epulonum*, who became seven (*septemuiri*) under Sulla, relieved the pontiffs of their task of organising the great banquets for the Capitoline triad and the Games. Their emblem was a *patera* (a shallow bowl used in ritual).

The public priests of Rome under the Empire

The major colleges

No change. All these priests celebrated the Games and the vows for the wellbeing of the emperor and his family on 3 January. Every 110 years, the *quindecemuiri* celebrated the Secular Games. The number of priests was increased only in exceptional circumstances, by one or two places. The minor *flamines* and minor pontiffs were now drawn from the equestrian order. ▶

▶ **The sodalities**

The sodalities of the cult of the deified emperors	25 in each sodality. The *sodales Augustales* (AD 14), who in 54 became the *sodales Augustales Claudiales*; the *sodales Flaviales Titiales* (81); the *sodales Cocceiani* (98), *Ulpiales* (118), *Hadrianales* (137); and, from 160 on, the *sodales Antoniniani*.	These celebrated the public cult of the deified emperors.
The Arval Brethren	12 members chosen by co-option with no popular participation. President: an annual *magister*, assisted by a *flamen*.	The brethren celebrated the sacrifice of Dea Dia at the ancient boundaries of the territory of Rome.
Sodales Titii (or *Titienses*)	20 (no other information)	(no information)
The priests of old Latin communities	The Laurentes Lavinates (Lavinium); the *sacerdotes* Albani (Alba); the Caeninenses (Caenina); the Tusculani (Tusculum); the Lanuvini (Lanuvium); the Suciniani (Sucinium). These priests bore the titles of magistrate, priest or sometimes citizen of the community concerned.	They celebrated the cults of the communities absorbed by the Romans or the cults shared by cities subject to Rome.

Under the Empire, the number of priests per college did not increase. From time to time supernumerary places were made available in the colleges for members of the ruling dynasty. The emperors regularly created new priesthoods, so the total number of public priests increased anyway. Under the Republic, priests were often co-opted before becoming members of the Senate. Under the Empire, the prestige of the great priesthoods led to stricter selection: generally, members of the major colleges were coopted around the age when they held the consulate – about 40 for non-patricians. Under Augustus and later, members of the four major colleges were regularly made responsible for new rituals: quinquennial Games for the wellbeing of the emperor under Augustus, and annual vows for the wellbeing of the emperor and his family.

2.2 The sodalities

The functions of sodalities were less wide-ranging and less important at the political level. Whereas the pontiffs, augurs and *(quin)decemuiri*, through their advice and their jurisdiction, exerted a direct influence on political and institutional life, the sodalities devoted themselves to particular ritual tasks. Their responsibilities did not extend beyond the celebration of a ritual or a festival. Unlike the Vestals, they were not even figures whose existence was seen, as it were, as a necessary condition for the existence of Rome. Because of their relative marginality, the sodalities did not evolve in the same way as the major colleges, hence they are often descibed as 'minor'. Untouched by the major priestly reforms of 300 and above all 104–103, they continued to bear witness to more ancient institutional forms.

In accordance with that tradition, the sodalities continued to recruit for themselves. The *nominatio* and co-option of new priests (which, for them, took the place of election) took place behind closed doors amongst the college members, with no intervention from the people. We know virtually nothing about these sodalities under the Republic. Some were so marginal (or aristocratic) that they may even have ceased to be active during the last two centuries of the Republic, or at least during the Civil Wars. But they were all resuscitated by Augustus, as models of an ancient form of priesthood, based originally on groups of aristocrats. Under the Empire, these sodalities both carried out the specific rituals for which they were responsible, and took part in the vows and sacrifices celebrated for the wellbeing of the emperor. As they were not subject to the prohibitions of priestly laws, these priesthoods could be combined with the major priesthoods.

The function of *fetiales* was to conclude treaties, denounce violations of them, insist on reparations and ritually transmit declarations of war. When on these missions, one of the priests was called the *pater patratus*, the other the *uerbenarius* (the bearer of ritual herbs?). We do not know what the function of the *fetiales* was under the Empire.

The *salii* sported an archaic warrior's uniform and carried shields and spears. Thus equipped, they paraded through the town at the opening (19 March) and the close (19 October) of the war season, singing a hymn of invocation to Janus, Jupiter, Juno, Minerva and Mars. Under the Empire, the *genius* of the reigning prince, the names of deified emperors and those of a few deceased members of the dynasty were included in this hymn. Augustus' name was added during his lifetime.

The *luperci* were responsible for celebrating the ritual of the Lupercalia (15 February), which included the sacrifice to Faunus of a ram and a dog, followed by a famous race round the Palatine run by priests clad in goat-skins.

The twelve Arval Brethren, resuscitated or reformed by Augustus in about 29/28 BC, celebrated the sacrifice to Dea Dia (in late May) and tended the goddess's grove.

On the *sodales Titienses* or *Titii*, who were probably likewise resuscitated by Augustus, nothing is known – except that there were twenty of them.

After Augustus' death, *sodales* devoted to the cult of deified or deceased members of the dynasty were created (twenty priests, and five members of the dynasty). The twenty-five *sodales Augustales* were appointed in AD 14. When Claudius died in 54, their services were extended to the deified Claudius and they were now known as the *sodales Augustales Claudiales*. In about 81, they were followed by the *sodales Flaviales Titiales* for the deified Vespasian and Titus, the *sodales Cocceiani Ulpiales Hadrianales* (whose name ended up simply as *Hadrianales*) for Nerva, Trajan and Hadrian, and finally the *Antoniniani*, after the deification of Antoninus Pius. After that, no more sodalities were created, but the nomenclature of the Antoniniani was altered at each new deification, when an extra *diuus* would be added to the priests' title.

There were also a number of priesthoods that carried out ancient rituals some of which originated from the conquest of Latium.

The *curiones*, who were of senatorial or equestrian rank, celebrated certain rites associated with the organisation of the thirty Roman *curiae* that they represented. In particular, they took part in the ritual of investiture for leading magistrates. Under the Republic, the Romans had celebrated a number of cults in common with the conquered Latin peoples, cults that the leading magistrates carried out every year (Juno Sospita in Lanuvium, the Penates and Vesta in Lavinium). During the Latin festivities on the Alban Mount, the leading magistrates, along with delegates from the thirty Latin cities, had to offer up a sacrifice to Jupiter Latiaris. These rites continued to be celebrated throughout the imperial period, but the role of the representatives of the Latin peoples was progressively taken over by Roman knights: colleges of priests composed of Roman knights were given the job of fulfilling the religious duties of ancient communities which, in many cases, had disappeared from Latium (Alba, Lavinium, Caerina, Tusculum, Lanuvium) or from Etruria (Sucinium), communities whose cults the Romans had amalgamated or whose duties they had absorbed. The best-known example is that of the Laurentes Lauinates, who replaced the people of Lavinium in the celebration of the rites shared between Lavinium and Rome and also at the annual re-enactment of the treaty concluded with the Romans in 338 BC. All these ancient priesthoods were linked with the institutional life of the ancient alliance between the Latins and Rome. Under the Empire, the opening up of the metropolis to citizens throughout the world was heralded – particularly at Lavinium and Alba – by these rituals and priesthoods (which were partly linked with the investiture of leading Roman magistrates) and by the myths woven around them.

2.3 The organisation of the priestly colleges

The priestly colleges, like the sodalities, were organised like Roman colleges in general. Their meetings took place in the same manner as the assemblies of any group. Generally, a *magister* ('superior') elected by the members of the college, presided, but sometimes his place was taken by a vice-president (*pro-magister*). The 'superior' of the pontiffs, the *pontifex maximus*, was elected directly by the people and his presidency was a life appointment. From the time of Augustus on, this extremely prestigious function was allotted to the emperor. In religious festivals celebrated by priests, authority was in many cases exercised by two individuals: one represented the active authority, and operated, as it were 'in real time' (he gave his name to the year, was elected, called meetings for his colleagues, and acted and issued decrees in their name); the other remained passive (dictated the formulae pronounced by the former, was present at the celebration of the ritual, and was 'taken' or 'seized' rather than elected). So, for example, we find the pontiff assisted by a *flamen* or by the Vestals, the *magister* of the Arvales side by side with a *flamen*, a *pater patratus* accompanied by a *uerbenarius*. In the rites celebrated by magistrates, it would be a pontiff or an augur who took the 'passive' role.

Every priestly college had an official headquarters, financial resources, and public slaves who performed administrative and ritual tasks. Every priest was also served by an assistant (*kalator*), usually one of his freedmen. These assistants also formed colleges and were responsible for managing the day-to-day affairs of their patrons and also for certain less central ritual tasks, such as expiations.

2.4 Election and co-option

Up until the second century BC, the priestly colleges co-opted their members. Later, their autonomy was reduced. Already by the end of the third century AD, the *pontifex maximus* was elected by the *comitia tributa* from three candidates put forward by the college of pontiffs. In 196, the same procedure was introduced for the *epulones*. After an initial setback in about 145, the system was extended to the three major colleges by the *Lex Domitia* of 104/103 BC. Every time a death occurred, each member of the college concerned had the right to propose (*nominare*) a candidate. It was then up to the *comitia tributa*, or rather a subsection of seventeen of its tribes chosen by lot before the vote, to elect (*creare*) the future priest from among the proposed candidates. Once elected, the future priest was co-opted (*cooptare*) by the college in question. Certain priests, such as augurs and *flamenes*, were also 'inaugurated'. Under the Empire, the elections of major priests evolved, along with the system of assemblies. From the reign of Tiberius(?) on, the *nominatio* and election took place in the Senate, but up until Domitian at least, every election was formally confirmed by a vote taken in the *comitia tributa*. *Flamines* and Vestals were 'seized' (*capere*) by the *pontifex maximus*. Under the Empire, when Augustus resuscitated the post of the *flamen* Dialis (of Jupiter), a number of rules determining the choice of these priests were reformed. However, the essential core of rules meanwhile remained in place, so it was hard to find candidates who satisfied all the requirements. To be a *flamen*, it was necessary to be married according to the ancient rite of *confarreatio*, which most of the leading families had abandoned. Besides, in order to supply candidates for all the patrician priesthoods, the emperors were regularly obliged to create new patricians, since the old families were dying out.

At the end of the Civil Wars, Octavian (the future emperor Augustus) received the right of proposing candidates for all vacant priestly posts and, as his candidates were never beaten, this gave him indirect control over the decisions of the colleges. Then, gradually, he himself came to be elected by all the colleges, which made it possible for him to dispense with that earlier right. Under the Republic, the accumulation of major priesthoods had been banned by the *Lex Domitia,* which had even tried to prevent two close relatives belonging to the same priestly college. But from Tiberius on, the emperor was *ex officio* elected and co-opted into all the colleges at his accession. He was thus in a position to control all priestly decisions.

Under the Republic, not all the priests in the major colleges had been of senatorial rank. By the end of that period all major priests were senators and rather less than half were patricians. It is not known what became of the traditional distribution of seats between patricians and plebeians under the Empire. The *rex sacrorum,* the major *flamines* and the *salii* were invariably of patrician rank, but we do not know enough about the rest of the priests to be able to check whether the tradition continued in the various colleges. Under the Republic, even though most priests were actually from senatorial or equestrian families, the choice of candidates was not formally limited to those two orders. Augustus reinforced the census qualification of priesthoods and of the priestly hierarchy. He made most of the important priesthoods senatorial and gave others (minor *flamines, luperci* and Latin priesthoods) equestrian rank.

3 OTHER PUBLIC PRIESTHOODS

3.1 The cults of Ceres, the Great Mother and Isis

Recruitment for the public priestess of Ceres (under the Republic, at least) had to be from 'foreigners', who were then given civic rights. We know nothing about the rules by which this priestess was governed. She was of lower social status than other priests. Likewise, we know virtually nothing about the high priests and priestesses of the Great Mother or the organisation of the *galli*. At the end of the reign of Antoninus Pius, an *archigallus* presided over them. The college of *dendrophori*, created under Claudius, and that of the *cannophori,* attested since the mid-second century, also participated in the cult of the Great Mother and Attis. The

Egyptian cults became part of Roman public cult under Caligula and later, above all, the Flavians, but the cult officials of Isis and Serapis were not incorporated into the system of public priesthoods. As well as the college of *pastophori*, who had administered the cult of Isis since the time of Sulla, and the *Anubo-* or *Bubastophori*, who had the right of carrying in procession the shrines with the insignia of the deities, there existed a numerous and specialised clergy (priests of Isis), over which a high priest (the 'prophet') probably presided.

3.2 The districts of Rome

The priesthoods of the various quarters of Rome were of lower rank, but had an important social function. The *magistri* and *flamines* of the *pagi* and the *montes* of the Republic were replaced, from 12 BC on, by *uicomagistri* and *uicoministri* (of servile rank) whose task was to celebrate the cult of the *Lares compitales*, later the *Lares Augusti*. Their colleges included free men, freedmen and slaves.

3.3 Colonies and municipia

The colonies and *municipia* had a simplified or less highly developed system of traditional Roman priesthoods. Under the Empire, alongside pontiffs and augurs (at least three in number) there might be found the *flamines* of deified emperors, priests of Rome and Augustus, and a few priesthoods of important local deities. At a lower level, the *Augustales* and *seuiri Augustales* (the number of whom varied) celebrated the same type of cults as the Roman *uicomagistri*. Finally, as the constitution of Colonia Genetiva (Urso) states, public temples and cults not managed directly by magistrates or priests were entrusted to annual *magistri*, appointed by the council of decurions.

Under the Empire, the conquest of the Mediterranean world and the organisation of the provinces gave rise to annual cults linking all the cities of a given province. These sent delegated representatives to a federal sanctuary where they took part in a great sacrifice addressed to Rome and Augustus. At this sanctuary the representatives each year elected the provincial priest, who directed the rites and sacrifices in question. The honour of being chosen as the delegate of their city and possibly being elected provincial priest represented the apex of the careers of members of the local elites. These sanctuaries and cults were developed first, from the time of Augustus on, in the Greek world, then likewise in the chief towns of all the provinces. According to a rescript of Constantine to the Hispellates (*CIL*, 11.5265), a similar system was set up in Italy at the time of the creation of judicial districts under Marcus Aurelius.

4 PRIVATE PRIESTHOODS

In families, it was the father or his representatives who carried out religious rituals. The head of the family fixed the calendar, decided which deities to honour, and celebrated the family festivals inside the home and at public cult sites. The greatest families had cults associated with their own 'clan' (*gens*), which from time to time reunited all those who claimed to belong to the same gens. Some of those cults may have been public. One such, some scholars think, was the cult of Hercules at the Great Altar, entrusted to the Potitii and the Pinarii until the city bought the priesthood in 312 BC. At a later date, the *gens Iulia* celebrated clan cults at Bovillae, ten miles out of Rome along the Via Appia; under the Empire, the cult of the imperial family (*domus Augusta*) was established at this spot.

Families would be surrounded by professional priests and priestesses who gravitated to them, offering their skills in divination or ritual for payment. *Haruspices*, astrologers, Chaldaeans, sorcerors, healers and *magi* were mocked and criticised, sometimes even persecuted, but everyone consulted them, the elite as well as the common people. In this type of priesthood, the priest would often be thought to be close to the deities and able to influence them, or even to bend them to his will, and the rites practised offered all the picturesque elements likely to impress the minds of his clients. The formulae and practices of these charlatans were not so very different from those in use in public or private cults. The cures recommended by Aesculapius, for example, resemble those of the healers who touted for custom at crossroads; and the venerable public rites of *deuotio* and the burial of living Gauls and Greeks were, in the last analysis, also magical rites of a spectacular kind. In 186 BC, traditional Bacchic rites were transformed by a Campanian priestess, in order to make a particularly powerful – and, in the view of the authorities, fraudulent – impact upon the initiates. A number of myths circulating in the Augustan period represented the Roman priests of archaic times as invested with extraordinary powers similar to those possessed by 'sorcerors', as if to stress the efficacy of the traditional rites and the power of priests.

Chapter 9

The double life of the Roman gods

The Romans, like the Greeks, accepted the fundamental principle that the gods lived in the world alongside men and strove with them, in a civic context, to bring about the common good. They also believed that the deities surpassed the city and its mortal inhabitants by far, in fact were awesomely superior. In religion, however, human relations with the immortals came down essentially to an image of deities who were close, benevolent, and unwilling to make use of their superhuman powers in day-to-day life. The gods did occasionally reveal their true faces, either in particular rituals or when they were angered; and then their language was one of cataclysms, epidemics and devastation – in short, terror. But in ordinary life, they did not behave as absolute masters and tyrants, but as fellow-citizens and benevolent patrons. They did not demand dishonourable behaviour or humiliating devotion from mortals and, above all, they did not attempt to control men's thoughts. In a passage discussing the behaviour one should adopt towards slaves, Seneca compares the gods to masters who act as patrons rather than as tyrants: 'They (slaves) ought to respect you rather than fear you . . . Some may say "This is what he plainly means: slaves are to pay respect as if they were clients or early-morning callers!" Anyone who holds this opinion forgets that what is good enough for a god cannot be too little for a master' (*Letters to Lucilius*, 47.18).

To be sure, the immortals had a right to the honours assigned to their extremely high rank in earthly society, but like other citizens of high rank – magistrates, senators and the other dignitaries of Roman society – they were not much concerned with the intentions of those who honoured them and were content simply to expect and receive the homage due to them. These basic theological principles were not expressed solely in philosophical speculations. All rituals that the Romans celebrated day by day constructed the image of the *citizen gods*.

1 CITIZEN GODS, PATRON GODS, TERRIFYING GODS

As we have seen in connection with the major religious rituals, the deities owed their place at the heart of cities not to any epiphany – not, that is, to any personal manifestation on their part – but above all to a human decision, the will of the people, the senate, a magistrate or a mythical king. Within the family context, it was the will of the *paterfamilias* that decided on the adoption of a deity by his domestic community. When an unknown deity unexpectedly manifested himself or herself, even with the purpose of coming to the Romans' aid, like the famous Aius Locutius in the fourth century BC, his epiphany had first to be accepted by the public institutions; it had to receive, as it were, the approval of a majority vote in the Senate. One Christian writer could write with irony: 'Among you (pagans) a god's divinity depends on man's decision. Unless a god please man, he shall not be a god at all; in fact, man must look kindly on god' (Tertullian, *Apologeticus* 5.1).

Once they were members of the community, the gods kept quiet. Implicitly, every ritual recognised the benevolent and ordered services that they rendered to the Roman people. Certainly, every ritual declared that Rome was ruled by the magistrates and the gods together. But to participate actively in public decisions and to intervene in the destiny of the Roman people, a deity had first to be formally 'seized upon' by the magistrates. Like their mortal 'colleagues', the senators, the gods had to be consulted in the manner that custom prescribed. They had to participate in the taking of a public decision but did not, *ex officio*, have the right to speak. Only when the magistrate had spoken could the gods respond. The gods – like the Senate, the priests and the assembly of the people – had to wait until the consul invited them to speak. And even then, they could not express their opinions freely: in general they were content to give a yes-or-no answer. For example, every time a law was passed by vote, an election took place, or a public decision was reached, Jupiter had to be consulted by taking the auspices. The rite clearly proclaimed Jupiter's rank, for he was expected to express himself before the other citizens and either authorise or not authorise the magistrate to proceed in his actions. The will of Jupiter was therefore superior to that of the Roman people. Does this mean that the sovereign god imposed his opinion and will upon the consuls? Not at all, at least not in normal times. As we have seen, in a consultation of the auspices, it was not the god who expressed himself: the consulting magistrate, helped by a few assistants, provided both the questions and the answers, to the point where both Cicero and Dionysius of Halicarnassus could conclude that the sign sought from the god could never have any meaning other than that which the magistrate ascribed to it. And even if Jupiter, exasperated by some tactlessness on the part of his fellow-citizens, manifested his irritation through a spontaneous and undeniable sign, it was still up to the magistrate in question to accept or reject it. Basically, it is fair to say that taking the auspices and the acceptance or rejection of an unexpected sign simply constituted a dramatic way of announcing that a decision taken in the name of the Roman people enjoyed the approval of the gods and did not violate their prerogatives. At the same time, these rituals, which could in no circumstances be omitted or taken lightly, tempered the power of a magistrate and forced him to take account of others who also communicated with Jupiter: his colleague or colleagues, the augur(s). So, despite appearances, the gods to some extent did control the power game, but they did so discreetly and were always represented by other human beings.

In any case, to get himself heard, the only option for Jupiter (or, come to that, for the mass of the Roman people) was secession and violent demonstration. Jupiter could reject his role of *patronus* of the Roman people and allow disasters to fall upon his 'clients'. Prodigies and catastrophes conveyed the gods' wrath to the magistrates and prompted them to seek the reason for it. For divine anger was caused by some offence, not by the tyrannical will of an absolute sovereign. It indicated some forgetfulness, an omission, an insult to the dignity of the deity, not a loss of faith: a magistrate had celebrated a rite incorrectly, or had forgotten to celebrate it, or had committed some sacrilege. An inquiry then established the cause of the anger and the breakdown of 'peace with the gods' (*pax deorum*) and prescribed the rituals designed to repair the offence, if necessary with the aid of the Sibylline Books. In this way, rituals associated with the anger of the gods allowed the Romans to account for their misfortunes in a rational way: it was a question of the public rituals being violated. Dramatic events of this kind also progressively helped them to glimpse their destiny. For it was at such times that the Romans regularly reflected upon and redefined the limits of their Empire and their interests, and introduced new deities into their 'pantheon'. This kind of reflection, also, would be initiated and controlled by a magistrate assisted by the Senate and the priestly colleges. In short, the example of divination in all its forms shows that, notwithstanding their superiority, in the city of Rome the gods were under the control of the magistrates. And this control could be every bit as binding as what was called in the Greek world *heimarmene*, the destiny imposed upon mortals and immortals alike. There can be no doubt that the power to converse with the gods, to request their advice and weigh it up, or – to be more precise – the power to speak for them, conferred an extraordinary prestige upon the Roman aristocrats.

Legitimate as it was, this power and this magisterial role were not unlike that sought by sorcerors and magicians. These claimed that, by powerful secret methods, they could establish with a deity an intimate relationship from which they themselves derived knowledge and power. But unlike the power of the magistrates, that of the sorcerors was considered ambiguous by their fellow-citizens, because they suspected that it had been obtained by force, with intent to do harm. The power that the magistrates brought to bear upon the immortals was, by contrast, regarded as the result of a pact freely concluded between the city's two partners, with a view to furthering the wellbeing of all. At any rate, when a Roman turned to a sorceror to resolve a problem, it was because he reckoned that the latter possessed direct access to a particular deity, access more reliable than the prayers and vows that one could make privately in a sanctuary.

The same image of the gods is conveyed by other practices we can observe, for example consecration. As we have seen, here too the decision of the magistrates and priests was paramount. We know that deities could be expelled from their sanctuaries if the state decided that it had another use for the space where they resided. All that was required was a rite of exauguration, evocation or liberation. Similarly, an object dedicated by private individuals, but not by public order, was not sacred. In their own way, customs such as these also defined the gods' status in the city.

But in the case of the residences of the gods, the traditions are richer. Although the temples and sanctuaries built by public decision fit in with this image of the deities, other types of sacred places do not: groves, deep caves, fathomless pools, the sources of rivers and so on. All these amazing natural phenomena were immediately stamped with the mark of divinity and they struck terror into mortal beings. In places such as these, the gods revealed their other face, the one that corresponded to their superhuman nature. But once again, by performing the appropriate rites it was possible for mortals to take over at least a part of these places – to establish a sanctuary there or to clear it for fields – an activity that seems to have been commemorated by the festival of the Lucaria (19 and 21 July).

It was not only in public religion that the tension between the two faces of the gods was evident. It was also clear in the religious practices of magicians and sorcerors, who used it to show their own power or the efficacy of their rites, by placing themselves or their clients in front of the 'true' face of the deity. The reformed Bacchic cult that became widespread at the beginning of the second century BC and provoked the scandal of the Bacchanalia (186 BC) also resorted to this way of representing relations with the gods. Dionysus played this role in the Greek world. Every year, his arrival on the day of his festival showed the other face of the gods, liberating citizens and their wives from all social rules and establishing an absolute power over them. This annual epiphany was an ancient venerable tradition, part of the legitimate public cults. According to our sources, until the second century there was nothing of the kind in Rome. But then it seems that the leaders of Bacchic communities used the terror aroused by direct contact with the deity to establish a hold over the minds of young Romans that the Roman authorities deemed criminal and accordingly repressed. Two centuries later, the clergy of Isis similarly abused the credulity of a *matrona* by leading her to believe that she was about to meet the god Serapis in person.

To be sure, it would not be too misleading to suggest that the elite also played upon the irrational fears of the common people, so as more easily to bend them to its will. But the same can be said of all religions. All are based on a deeply rooted conviction in people's minds (*all* minds) that the gods exist and that one needs to behave in accordance with that reality. Roman tradition on the relationship of humans with the gods set the highest value on reason, the sense of law so characteristic of a civic culture. In this context terror before the immortals played a marginal role. That, at least, was what the rituals and the theological treatises proclaimed. For this religion and the elite that controlled it were, in fact, struggling against an irrational terror of the gods and superstition, far more than they were using that terror in order to govern more easily.

2 FUNCTIONS, HIERARCHIES, COLLABORATIONS

So far we have approached the gods in a very general way, either as the 'patrons' of the Romans or, on the contrary, as terrifyingly superior immortals. However, the rituals and customs of the Romans tell us much more about divine nature. They show that the Roman gods are innumerable, that each has a function and a precise profile, and that, individually, they are not all-powerful. This is a polytheistic system and, despite those who see an evolutionary progression from polytheism to monotheism, its deities were not moving towards monotheism. Even religious currents linked with deities of creation, or superior in some other sense, accept the existence of other deities. Gods such as Isis and Baal, supreme within their own religious systems, were venerated as such in Rome; this, as long as those cults lasted, made it possible to experiment with a different type of relationship with the divine and between gods. Even as late as the fifth century, Christian thinkers, ardent defenders of monotheism, could still not get rid of the mass of 'pagan' gods. They ridiculed them but placed them among the demons.

2.1 The profiles of the Roman gods

Each of the Roman gods possessed a precise profile. The term '*the* sacred', in the modern sense, meant nothing to the Romans; and no more did the abstract notion of '*the* divine'. The once heated debate over the Latin term *numen* is now over. Nowadays nobody considers, as did the 'primitivists' (Ludwig Deubner, Herbert J. Rose, and their successors) that *numen* means 'a diffused sacredness'. Instead, *numen* is now translated, depending on the context, as the 'will or power of a deity'. And the formula, or rather the deity, *Siue deus siue dea* ('god-or-goddess') that used to be invoked in support of the theory of a 'diffused sacredness' is now interpreted quite differently; it is now believed to have constituted a precaution designed not to offend a deity whose name was unknown because he or she was a foreigner and was not yet revealed to the Romans. So this was not a deity that was both 'god-*and*-goddess', but simply one that was either 'god-*or*-goddess'. The terms ('god'/'goddess') are exclusive and do not convey the sexual indifferentiation supposedly characteristic of a primitive representation of the divine.

As the Romans saw it, there were countless gods. They filled the whole known world. Some had made themselves known to the Romans, bore a traditional name, possessed a residence and a cult. These were part of the Roman public or private order. Other deities lived in foreign lands. If the Romans were active in those lands it seemed to them inevitable that they should enter into relations with these, either setting up a cult for them on the spot, or inviting them to take up residence in Rome. Moreover, even in Roman territories, certain deities were presumed to be present, even if they had not deemed it necessary to reveal themselves to the Romans. This is a very interesting category of deities, for it throws light on the Romans' concept of the gods. When faced with a serious situation, for example a war or the destruction of a religious site, the vows that were expressed and the expiatory sacrifices that were offered were targeted at all the deities involved in the event in question. We thus learn that, as well as the patron deity of a particular sanctuary and the other gods and goddesses who helped to manage it or assisted the patron deity in their function, the place might also contain other deities, such as the famous 'god-or-goddess' who, in one document, is even accompanied by another 'god-or-goddess-who-protects-this-place'. We also discover that deities, even the greatest of them, cannot do everything. So, according to the vows formulated when Emperor Trajan went off to war on 25 March 101, the Capitoline triad helped the emperor to return victorious, but to make it quite clear that it was no less than victory that the Romans were expecting, a special prayer was addressed to 'Jupiter the victor'. Mars the victor was also invoked; and so that there should be no doubt at all, a third deity, whose very name expressed the result expected from the support of Mars – Victoria.

A selection of the public Roman deities

Deity	Function	Epithet	Patronage
Jupiter	Sovereignty	*Optimus maximus* (the best, the greatest)	The state
Juno	Defence, childbirth	*Regina, Lucina*	The state, women
Minerva	Technology		The state, artisans, doctors
Aesculapius	Healing		Doctors
Apollo	Good order, purification, prophecy	*Medicus*	
Bellona	The efforts of war		
Bona Dea	Healing		*Matronae*
Carmenta	Inspired speech		Women
Castores (Castor and Pollux)	Warrior activities		Knights
Ceres	Growth	Mater (venerable)	*Matronae*
Consus	Storage		
Dea Dia	Clear light		Harvests
Diana	Procreation	(*Nemorensis*)	Women
Dis pater	Underworld		
Dius Fidius	Oaths		
Faunus	Borders of cultivated land		
Fides	Good faith		
Flora	Flowering		

Fons (m.)	Springs		
Fortuna	Chance	(Many)	Slaves, women
Genius (or Juno for women)	The power of action of an individual, thing or place	(Constructed with the genitive of the being in question)	Individuals, communities, places
Great Mother	Warding off catastrophes in this life	Idean, Cybele	Romans– 'Trojans', workers in wood
Hercules	Success in heroic activities	*Victor* (victorious)	Entrepreneurs
Isis	Safety	(Many)	Sailors
Janus	Beginnings	*Pater* (venerable)	
Juturna	Clean water		Water suppliers
Lares	Areas of land		
Liber	Germination	*Pater* (venerable)	(Adolescents)
Mars	Warrior violence	Pater (venerable)	Army
Mercury	Journeys		Merchants
Mithras	Hope of support, especially in this life	Inuictus (unconquered)	The military, imperial employees
Neptune	Underground streams, the sea	Pater (venerable)	Seafarers
Ops	Abundance		
Pales (f.)	The health of flocks		Shepherds
Portunus	Reaching land	*Pater* (venerable)	
Proserpina	Underworld		
Quirinus	Civic community		The people
Robigo	Wheat-rust		

Salus	Physical and moral welfare	(Public)	
Saturnus	Unbinding, loosening		
Silvanus	The wild	*Sanctus* (pure)	Slaves
Tellus	Place of growth		
Venus	Irresistible charm	*Victrix, genetrix* (victorious, mother)	Couples, Romans
Vesta	Hearth	*Mater* (venerable)	Romans
Volturnus	Tiber?		
Vulcan	Dangerous fire		Ostia

Roman polytheism was not solely based on the fact that there were innumerable gods. Rather, its principle lay in the limitation of divine functions and the ability of human beings to increase the number of gods by constantly splitting up the actions attributed to them. At any rate, a deity possessed or was given divine colleagues, helpers and servants (*ministri* – the term goes back to Augustine) in order to cover a wider field of action. Making divine the deity's 'power of action' (*numen*) represented the abstract side to this process. The world of the gods was thus indefinitely extendable yet could, at the same time, be reduced to just a few units, depending upon whatever was needed. Very little information exists to help us to understand the reasons and rules that dictated an increase or a decrease in the number of gods in different contexts. In a way, this was what piety was all about: skilfully seeking out all the deities involved in a particular situation, knowing all the deities implicated in a particular action. The theology spelt out by ritual might thus be defined as a traditional kind of speculation on the mysteries of action. What is certain is that this mass of gods both great and small did not represent – as has sometimes been argued – an accumulated historical silt, a fossilised remnant left by an evolution from functional gods to personal ones. Quite simply, this was how polytheism normally worked.

2.2 The functions of the Roman gods

Each of the deities possessed a precise function (sovereignty, technology, warrior violence, plant growth, etc.) and exercised this in a wide variety of fields. Georges Dumézil has shown that in Rome the fundamental nature of Mars was no different when he mounted guard on the edge of a field or the edge of a (state) territory; he had simply moved from one place to another. There was nothing to prevent him defending the people or an individual against an aggressive disease, but that did not make him a god who specialised in healing and the pursuit of physical wellbeing. He simply remained the violent defender of the people as a whole or of the individual. So it is perfectly logical that Roman deities are never on their own. Very rarely does one come across a ritual or a sanctuary in which a deity is invoked in isolation. In the functional polytheism of the Romans, the gods stand side by side and collaborate with one another. This is why it is always dangerous to assimilate one deity to another, as if they were to all intents and purposes the same. For such assimilation tends to deny the particular distribution of divine functions as it is evidenced in ritual. The speculations on the ultimate nature of the divine in which philosophers of antiquity sometimes indulged have nothing to do with the Roman religion of ritual and sanctuaries and amount rather to an attempt to reduce polytheism to monotheism. The same applies to many superficial modern studies of female deities, which often present them as more or less interchangeable mother-goddesses or fertility goddesses. Fertility is, in any case, a concept so vague and so general that it could well encompass the whole of religion and all the deities. But what else could one expect of such a vague concept? How could it possibly help to reconstruct and understand rites very few of which explicitly evoke 'fertility'? To be sure, people approached a whole number of deities in their quest for children, for a good harvest and for the reproduction of their herds, but to reduce religion to those requests is to oversimplify what was at stake and what was expected. The religion of the ancients was not just a matter of harvest festivals and festivities to celebrate sowing and reproduction. Above all, such a levelling down of functions destroys the essential kernel of the cult: the ritual construction of the world of the gods, in short the very essence of Roman polytheism.

Associations between deities could be either temporary, such as those mentioned above, or else permanent. Some cults and sanctuaries incorporated two or three titular deities. The temple on the Capitol provided a home for Jupiter, Juno and Minerva, each in a separate *cella*; and, near the Forum Boarium, twin sanctuaries were dedicated to Mater Matuta and Fortuna. But it is not certain whether associations such as these remained unchanged. According to the ancients, the first Capitoline triad consisted of Jupiter, Mars and Quirinus, and this is indeed attested by both rituals and myth. Furthermore, a 'divine court' always surrounded the main patron deity of a sanctuary. Some of these guest deities helped the principal deity to carry out his or her function correctly, to see that that the cult was properly conducted (in particular Vesta and Janus) and to manage the cult site. Other deities were invited for their prestige. Jupiter, for instance, might be associated with a cult for honorific reasons. Under the Empire, the situation became even clearer when the *genius* of the emperor and the deified emperors were honoured at the same time as the patron deities of other temples: such associations were expressed by the construction of secondary shrines and altars in most cult sites.

3 *DIUI*, THE *GENIUS* OF AUGUSTUS, THE *NUMEN* OF AUGUSTUS AND THE 'CULT OF THE EMPERORS'

3.1 Diui and diuae

After Caesar's assassination, within a few decades it became customary to elevate emperors on their death to the level of the gods – or, to be more exact, of the demi-gods. Julius Caesar was deified by a law that laid down divine honours for the dead man. Under the Empire, the Senate announced the apotheosis of Augustus on the day after his funeral. Once deified, the deceased could no longer receive funerary honours, nor could his image be carried in funeral processions. Before the reign of Caligula, deification was restricted to emperors, that is to say those known as 'Augustus'. In fact, before AD 38 only Augustus and had been deified; Tiberius had been denied the honour; Caligula's sister, Drusilla, was next. Under the Principate of Augustus, an intermediate category had been created for deceased princes, in particular for the young Caesars, Gaius and Lucius (AD 2 and 4), Germanicus (19) and Drusus (23). Their funerals were solemnly celebrated and an official annual funerary cult was addressed to them. Furthermore, their images were carried, along with those of deities, in the processions for the opening of the Games, their names were cited in prayers, and the so-called 'prerogative' *centuriae* of the *comitia centuriata* were called after them. All these honours raised the dead princes above the ordinary dead, but did not quite turn them into *diui*. After the deification of Drusilla, the honours of apotheosis were also conferred upon members of the imperial family, their children and close relatives.

Diui and *diuae* who received cults in Rome (44 BC–AD 240)

Julius Caesar
Augustus
(Drusilla)
(Livia)
Claudius
(Claudia Augusta, daughter of Nero)
(Poppaea Augusta)
Vespasian
Titus

▶

▶ (Julia Augusta, daughter of Domitian)
Nerva
(Marciana Augusta, sister of Trajan)
Trajan
(Matidia, mother-in-law of Hadrian)
Plotina, wife of Trajan
Hadrian
Sabina, wife of Hadrian
Faustina, wife of Antoninus
Antoninus
Lucius Verus
Faustina, wife of Marcus Aurelius
Marcus Aurelius
Commodus
Pertinax
Septimius Severus
M. Antonius (Caracalla)
Julia Domna
Severus Alexander
(Julia Maesa)

(List established on the basis of the evidence of the Arval Brethren. The *diuae* with names in parenthesis are not specifically named in the inscriptions but are included to make up the total number of *diui* and *diuae* to that indicated by the inscriptions.)

Diui and, after Matidia, *diuae* were allotted a temple, a *flamen*, *sodales* and a public cult. This was celebrated on the anniversary of the dedication of their temples (for example, 18 August for the deified Julius), the anniversary of their apotheosis (17 September for Augustus), or on anniversaries of their great exploits (for example, in the case of Augustus, the capture of Alexandria on 1 August, or his return from the east during the Augustalia of 12 October) or simply on their birthdays. The cult of these *diui* was celebrated not only in Rome but throughout the Western provinces, in the cities and in their provincial *consilia*. In the Greek world, honours equivalent to those of the gods were offered to the living emperor. The forms of the cult varied according to the rank of the city: they were not necessarily the same in the Roman colonies and the *municipia* as they were in foreign (*peregrini*) cities, for the latter were totally free to organise their cults as they wished. In provincial cults and in cities of the Empire, worship of Augustus was generally associated with worship of Rome (the goddess Roma), but in some places shrines gathered together the whole imperial family or all the deified emperors.

After the deification of Severus Alexander, between 235 and 238, apotheosis continued to be granted to emperors and empresses right down to Theodosius, provided, that is, they did not suffer the reverse and their memory was not 'damned' (subject to *damnatio memoriae*).

3.2 The Genius of the emperor

The cult of the *diui* was not the only one that related to the emperor. In Rome and in Latin-speaking countries, there were also other cult figures. By the beginning of the Principate of Augustus, sacrifices were offered to the *genius* of Augustus, a personification of his innate qualitites. The cult of a *genius* was a traditional cult that could relate to individuals as well as to things or places (see below). The *genius* of Augustus (or of *the* Augustus, the 'August One') was represented dressed in a toga with the features of the emperor in question and carrying a horn of plenty (*cornucopia*) and a *patera* (offering bowl). Gradually it also become customary to venerate the 'Juno' of the empress, represented as a *matrona* carrying a horn of plenty. Creating this kind of cult, extended to the public persona of the emperor domestic forms of cult (such as that of the *genius* of the *paterfamilias*), or forms previously reserved for particular Roman surroundings (the *genius* of Rome or some other place). Augustus exploited this ambiguity, for he was always keen to resort to categories of the family and to the symbolism of the powers of the *paterfamilias* in order to define his own relations with the citizens. The Roman people also celebrated the anniversaries and birthdays of the emperor's family, the *domus Augusta*, and the major events associated with it.

After 12 BC, when Augustus was elected *pontifex maximus*, he reintroduced the cult of the Compitalia, which had been banned since the fifties BC (or rather, he allowed the celebration of the Games linked to this cult). Between 12 and 2 BC he created sanctuaries at the crossroads (*compita*) in every district of Rome (Pliny cites 265 of them). These were designed to contain statues of the two Lares Augusti and also one of the *genius* of Augustus. The Lares were the deities of an area of land, or in this case the town district; but by slightly twisting the scholarly interpretation which suggested that the Lares were also the spirits of the dead, the implicit message was that this crossroads cult was addressed to the deceased members of Augustus' family. In this way the latter were elevated above the ordinary dead, at least in the minds of Romans capable of appreciating this kind of interpretation – that is to say, the Roman elite. The cult was entrusted to annually appointed *uicomagistri* chosen from the elite of the district concerned, who were assisted by *uicoministri*, of servile rank. This cross-roads cult, celebrated at the time of the Compitalia, in early January, was the public cult of the Roman town districts and promoted the cohesion and self-esteem of the local inhabitants. By once again allowing the town quarters to celebrate their own cults and games, and even providing them with shrines, Augustus was deliberately promoting his own popularity at the same time as spreading new forms of public cult. A similar type of cult was introduced in the colonies and *municipia*, where *Augustales* and *seuiri Augustales* were made responsible for the cult of the *Lares Augusti*. The ancient *Augustales* were generally of modest origin but nevertheless constituted an order that ranked immediately below the *decuriones* in the local community. However, they could not aspire to celebrate the public imperial cult of a city: that was a role that fell to the *flamen* of Augustus (and of Rome) or else to the local magistrates.

3.3 The numen

The famous name of 'Augustus' was in theory linked to the domain of the sacred. The adjective 'august' designated 'the full supernatural power' possessed by a sign sent by Jupiter or some other deity (as in the term *augustum augurium*). Without turning him into a god, this epithet too elevated him above other mortals by underlining the quasi-divine good fortune that he had displayed in the Civil Wars. One particular cult underlined this extraordinary capability. As soon as the name Augustus was introduced, the cult of the *numen* of Augustus began to spread. This cult of the divine power of Augustus (or the 'August One') was combined in Roman cities and in the provinces with a cult devoted to Rome and Augustus. Like the 'constitutional settlement' of 27 BC which gave Augustus power equivalent to the Roman people's (though without substituting his power for theirs), the cult of Rome-and-Augustus granted the emperor the same honours as those of the goddess who personified Rome. Similar reasons prompted the introduction into the hymn of the *salii* of the names of emperors and a few of their intended (but prematurely deceased) heirs, and also the annual proclamation of public vows for the wellbeing of the emperor and his family (on 3 January), vows similar to those aiming for the wellbeing of the *respublica* (1 January). It should be emphasised, however, that all these privileges were invented gradually over a period covering half a century, and were instituted either by a law or by a *senatusconsultum*, often in response to considerable popular pressure. Moreover, some of them were declined by Augustus.

3.4 The 'imperial cult'

The partisans of Augustus were, without doubt, behind the introduction of these religious novelties and privileges, but it should not be forgotten that the birth of what is called the 'imperial cult' (quite improperly, as the emperor was never officially venerated as a god during his lifetime) was not promoted and imposed solely from above. Recent research has shown that this worldwide movement frequently originated among the people, in the cities and provinces – for it offered a way, through religion, of conceptualising the development and success of an altogether new type of political power. In Rome itself, the origin of this movement was no different. Following the rule, instituted right at the beginning of the Principate, that nobody could hold greater power or honours than those of Augustus, the emperor and his family were granted honours equal to those enjoyed by the gods. The motive of this elevation, in Rome, in Italy and in the provinces alike, was a desire to define in this way the exceptional power gathered into the hands of Augustus and his successors. It was power that could be understood and thought of as the epiphany of a divine power in the hands of a mortal.

4 DOMESTIC AND FAMILY DEITIES

4.1 The Lares

Every family (*domus*) honoured its own gods, some of which went by the same name everywhere (the Lares, the *genius*, the Penates), while the names of others depended on particular family traditions. Thus each family honoured its own Lar (in Greek, *heros*), the deity that protected the land on which the family lived. As well as regular worship (on the Kalends, the Nones and the Ides of the month), the Lar received offerings at all family feasts and banquets. Up to the beginning of the common era, the Lar was addressed in the singular but, no doubt under the influence of the *Lares Augusti*, the plural of the word later came to be used. In their domestic shrines (*lararia*) set up in the communal rooms of homes, the Lares, from the beginning of the Empire on, were represented as two young men dancing and pouring wine from a horn into a *patera*. The cult of the Lares involved the entire household, the slaves as well as the *domus*.

4.2 The *genius*

Much the same applies to the cult of the *genius* of the *paterfamilias*. The *genius* (in Greek, *daimon* or *tukhe*) was the personification of the active force of a being, a thing or a place, as it was constituted at the moment of its birth or creation. To judge by the *lararia* of Pompeii and according to certain stories, the *genius* of a place or a person could be represented by a snake; but it was also represented as a man dressed in a toga, sometimes carrying a horn of plenty and a *patera*. In a domestic context, people swore by the *genius* of the *paterfamilias* and honoured that *genius* on the birthday of the master of the house. Around the beginning of the Empire, it became customary also to revere the Juno of the mistress of the house, the feminine equivalent of a *genius*. Gods and goddesses, we should not forget, likewise possessed a *genius* or a Juno.

4.3 The Penates and other domestic deities

Alongside the Lares and the *genius*, the Penates were also honoured. These were in some senses vague deities lodged in the innermost part of a house, but they could be separated out into a number of individual deities particularly revered by the family. To judge from the evidence of Pompeii, they would number between two and eight and sometimes included some of the major gods. Vesta, the hearth goddess, had no cult place of her own in households, except possibly in the flames of a sacrifice or those of the cooking fire. Nor did the Roman colonies and *municipia* have sanctuaries for Vesta: clearly the only hearth that really mattered to Roman citizens was that of the Roman Forum.

It was not unknown for particular family members to be deified after death. Cicero commented ironically on Caesar's apotheosis, but thought seriously of deifying his daughter Tullia. His project was no fancy, for in Rome (*CIL*, 6.7581) and also in the provinces (*CIL*, 13.8705, Upper Germany) we know of inscriptions that attest the private deification of dead women.

Leading families also maintained cults that extended beyond the family context. They were responsible for the upkeep of local or even public temples situated on their land, which they had to throw open to all on the god's festival day. The myth of the Potitii and the Pinarii, the two families in charge of the Ara Maxima (in the Forum Boarium), provides a clear picture of the situation. The old families of the Roman aristocracy thus celebrated what were known as family (gentilician) cults, as they involved a whole *gens*, but which were nevertheless public. The best-known are the family cult of the *gens* Julia (Venus, Veiovis) and that of the *gens* Aurelia (Sol).

4.4 The Di manes, *funeral ceremonies and the cult of the dead*

Another type of domestic cult, whose correct celebration was of concern to the whole community, was the funerary cult. In every family, the father or son buried the family dead. In a ceremony observed by more or less all families, the bodies of the deceased were taken to a cemetery situated outside the city, stretching along the roads leading out of town and particularly clustering near the gates. At country houses, the cemetery was found at the boundary of the occupied land or at the side of a nearby road. The funeral rites were celebrated in the necropolis, in front of the tomb. The reasons determining the general trends of the changing mortuary practices are not clear. After a period in archaic times when cremation was favoured, the prevailing fashion in the sixth century BC came to be burial. In the first century BC, cremation again became widespread – before giving way to burial once more in the second half of the second century. These variations did not depend on any particular shift in belief, but were somehow linked to developments within traditional practice. In any case, the various changes may be less significant than they seem, given that, even in cases of cremation, it was still customary to bury what was left of the body, so that a tomb existed according to sacred law. All that changed was the way of destroying the corpse and reducing it to imperishable bones. Sometimes that task was left to fire, sometimes to the earth. We should remember that cremation, even if just a symbolic cremation (when, for example, the body had actually been cremated abroad), was always a central element in the funerals of emperors. Elsewhere, in the provinces, funeral procedures varied.

At any rate, it was the funeral ritual that transformed the corpse, whether cremated or not, into one of the deceased. It went to join the *di manes*. These existed as a group, but were generally invoked as the *di manes* of some particular individual, as can be seen from countless tomb inscriptions. The funerary sacrifice offered in front of the funeral pyre (or the open tomb in cases of burial) proclaimed the new status of the dead person. The victim (usually a pig) and the offerings made to the deceased and to his *manes* (wine, oil, perfumes) were burnt in a holocaust on the pyre or in a fire next to the tomb. The relatives of the deceased did not share this meal, thereby marking the distance that now separated them from the dead. The grieving family, for its part, seems to have sacrificed to the Penates and then eaten their share of this sacrifice. In this way, the first meal that the deceased consumed took the form of smoke, as it did for the gods. Where there was a cremation, the symbolism was even clearer, since the body itself was transformed by the same fire that made the foodstuffs edible for the immortals. Meanwhile the mortals ate the meat that was their share of the victim offered to the Penates. When the fire was extinguished, the bones and ashes were collected up, washed in wine, and placed in an urn, which was deposited in the tomb. At different periods, a variety of offerings might accompany this burial: personal objects, or crockery used in the banquet, as a sign of the status of the deceased; and rites were probably performed annually, to confirm that status.

During the communal festival of the dead (the Parentalia, 13–22 February) and on particular anniversaries, a family would gather by the tomb and offer a sacrifice on the ground, in front of it. The 'pyre' on which the sacrifice was burnt as a holocaust recalled the pyre of the day of the funeral. Offerings took a variety of forms, ranging from a cup of wine to an animal victim, and generally included libations of perfume (which explains the glass and earthenware flasks often found in tombs) and wreaths. Some tombs were equipped with channels that made it possible to pour libations straight into the interior.

During the period of mourning, the family of the dead person was considered 'soiled' (*funestatus*) and its members adopted a degraded and dishevelled appearance. They wore dark clothes and stopped combing their hair and shaving, and carried out no public functions. But once the funeral rites had been celebrated, the mourning family gradually returned to normal life. On the eighth day a banquet, the *nouemdialis cena*, brought together the relatives and their guests. In leading families, the guests might include the whole Roman people and the banquet would be extremely lavish, even accompanied by gladiatorial games. During the festival of the dead, in February, the entire town went into mourning for ten days, for all the citizens had their own dead to commemorate and all, in their own ways, celebrated a funeral sacrifice such as that described above.

The dead who had not been buried in accordance with the rules, in particular those who had not been buried at all, were supposed to be dangerous for the living. In the month of May, a special festival was consecrated to them (the Lemuria, 9, 11 and 13 May). The father of the family offered their wandering spirits (*lemures*) a minimal banquet without any attempts at communication. At midnight, he tossed some beans over his shoulder, declaring 'By the beans I redeem myself and my family.'

This set of rites varied from one period to another, and from one place to another. Only the obligation to bury one's dead, according to the official rules, applied to one and all. But although the ritual was very similar for all families, particularly in the same period and the same region, it was never absolutely identical. Each *paterfamilias* decided for himself which customs to observe and, in doing so, would obey family traditions rather than prescriptions laid down by the priests. Because these rituals produced countless variants while remaining within the framework of a common tradition, there is very little explicit information on funerals and the festivals of the dead. As a result, many aspects of the cult of the dead are still unclear. The public decisions taken on the occasions of the funerals of Gaius Caesar and Lucius Caesar (AD 2 and 4) and of Germanicus (19) recorded in recently discovered inscriptions are therefore particularly precious, for they illuminate many aspects of the funeral rites.

PART V

Exegeses and Speculations

Chapter 10
Interpretations of Roman religion

The religious system of the Romans was founded on ritual, not on dogma. Their religious tradition prescribed rituals, not what they should believe. So each individual remained free to understand and think of the gods and the world-system just as he or she pleased. However, this does not mean that the authorities never went in for interpreting cult and the relations between human beings and their gods. They did indeed sometimes do so, but the purpose of these exegeses was neither to 'convert' those who did not 'believe' nor to produce dogmatic revelations about the world beyond. Rather, they prompted subjects for reflection which, at a religious festival or on a stroll through a cult site, might steer citizens' thoughts in a particular direction – always supposing they allowed themselves to reflect and to be open to such influence. In any case, the individual was no more obliged to believe in such or such an interpretation than in the cult itself. As we have seen, the only religious 'belief' for Romans consisted in the knowledge that the gods were the benevolent partners of mortals in the management of the world, and that the prescribed rituals represented the rightly expected coun-terpart to the help offered by the immortals. Nevertheless, all these approaches to the divine were closely linked, even if there was a separation in this religious system between belief and religious practice; and even if, up until the third century AD, the prevailing norm placed more value on practice at the expense of any personal research into the deity, opposing free and rational piety (*religio*) to irrational submission to the gods (*superstitio*).

It would be a huge undertaking to write a history of the Roman interpretation of religion. Within the framework of this book it is possible to indicate only a few elements. The fact is that religious interpretation is hard to disentangle from the history of philosophy, the sciences or literature. By following a traditional definition, popularised by Varro, we may divide Roman discourse on religion and the gods into three sections: civic, philosophical and mythological:

> It is recorded that the learned pontiff Scaevola maintained that three kinds of gods are handed down to us: one by the poets, another by the philosophers, and a third by the statesmen. He says that the first class is mere rubbish, because the poets invent many disgraceful stories about the gods; the second is not suited to city-states, because it includes some superfluous doctrines and some also that it is harmful for people to know.
>
> Augustine, *City of God*, 4.27 = Varro,
> *Divine Antiquities*, fr. 7, ed. Cardauns

It is often hard to distinguish the different genres of interpretation because they mostly appear in the same texts. For reasons of clarity, they will be grouped here under two headings.

1 CIVIC THEOLOGY

This type of interpretaton, the only type according to Varro and Cicero that could be defended without hesitation, was founded solely upon the religious institutions of the city. It can be divided into two broad approaches and two periods. The first is what can be deduced from practice, forming the background to priestly documents and prescriptions and the laws relating to religion. The second, inspired by Hellenistic thought, developed in the course of the last two centuries of the Republic and has the air of a civic 'science of religions'.

1.1 Traditional exegeses

Most of the ideas used and explained earlier in this book fall into this category, for they have been inferred from the general principles that governed religious practice. The Roman authorities (magistrates, Senate, priests), faced with the need to produce religious rules, devoted considerable reflection to relations with the gods. For example, at the time of the birth of the city, between the sixth and fifth centuries BC, when the magistrates and priests decided that any individual who offended the gods became impious and could no longer take part in collective life, they applied to this type of offence the kind of remedy for injury practised in conflicts between mortals; that is, they recognised the offended deity's right to take revenge and surrendered to him the person responsible for the transgression. The next step was taken when jurists drew a distinction between deliberate and involuntary impiety, and allowed any careless individual guilty of the latter to make reparation for the offence perpetrated. With this type of distinction, which was handed down to posterity by a judicial opinion of the *pontifex maximus* Quintus Mucius Scaevola, the city – while carefully scrutinising the guilty party's degree of culpability – deferred divine justice and obliged (so to speak) the offended deity to adopt a course of action founded upon reason.

The reasoning that guided those who elaborated all these categories was inspired by an image of the gods quite separate from that of deities who made the most of their superiority to tyrannise human beings. The civic image of 'citizen gods' was confirmed by numerous rituals and rules, and may be regarded as one of the major interpretations of traditional Roman religion. The determination, affirmed ever since at least the fifth century BC, to diminish the power of the priests and submit religion to the will and control of the people, expressed, for example, in laws relating to priesthoods, underlines the public and communal nature of the relationship between gods and men. It is reasonable to assume that this tendency was also linked with the contrast drawn between the kind of religion worthy of a citizen, on the one hand, and super-stition, on the other. At another level, the documents relating to sacrificial rituals regularly emphasised the traditional meaning of sacrifice, seen as a banquet held in common, which set in place the order of both the city and the world.

This traditional exegesis, for the most part no more than implicit, determines all decisions relating to religion as well as the interpretation of oracles. It constitutes the guiding thread running right through the corpus of sacred law and serves as a point of reference for all traditional discourse on religious matters. All these opinions put together may be regarded as the unwritten theology of the Romans: a 'science' of the gods expressed solely through this or that rule, or this or that allusion invoked in the debate. It was, in fact, formulated only when it was a matter of reforming or clarifying an element in the tradition, and its formulation did not extend beyond that particular point of detail. Sacred law, like all Roman law, was essentially a matter of custom and jurisprudence. Unfortu-nately for historians, the Roman system of religion and of sacred law had changed by the time their classical jurispru-dence was committed to writing, at the end of antiquity. As a result, most of the traditional religious 'doctrine' has been lost, and we are obliged to turn to other types of sources for information.

1.2 The birth of a 'science of religions'

Inspired by Hellenistic scholarship, in the third century BC the Romans began to reflect systematically upon their tradi-tions. Alongside the collections of facts that they extracted from priestly documents, they made use of existing religious institutions in a bid to reconstruct the origins of their rituals and to look beyond what was there to be seen and discover the ultimate nature of Roman traditions. One of the most favoured methods adopted in these speculations was etymol-ogy. This was pursued according to two basic principles. The one, introduced by Aelius Stilo, Varro's teacher, traced all words back to Latin, while the other, represented by the grammarians Hypsicrates and Cloatius Verus (first century BC), derived the origins of words from Greek, which made it easier to postulate a Greek origin for the Roman people. The etymological efforts of the ancients should not be measured by the yardstick of present-day linguistics or regarded as pure fantasy. Their interest and objective differed from those of modern linguists and historians. Through an etymological inquiry, Roman scholars hoped to reach out to a different reality, to the ultimate reason for things, which they frequently related to philosophical systems. At the same time, plenty of ancient etymologies constituted a minimal form of myth and functioned according to the same principles. We should therefore take care as we analyse the etymologies presented by the ancients, for even if they seem absurd to us today, they may contain a whole series of hints as to the way in which the ancients understood a particular institution.

The fact that antiquarians and etymologists in most cases ascribe conflicting etymologies to the same term is not surprising. In these researches it was a matter not of belief, but of speculative reflection; and furthermore the interpretation was not necessarily expected to produce a perfect coherence. The aim in view in these speculations was an abundance of propositions rather than the elimination of 'false' explanations. These series of interpretations should therefore be regarded as a rich source of information and each should be analysed in relation to the rest.

Unfortunately, few of these etymological works and dictionaries have survived. The work of Nigidius Figulus (early first century BC) is lost, but that of Varro is partially preserved. Cicero, Livy, Ovid, Verrius Flaccus (preserved in the form of a summary established in the second century by Festus), Dionysius of Halicarnassus, Plutarch and, later, Macrobius and Servius have all handed down many items of information, many of them gleaned from Varro. Together with the series of treatises that Cicero composed on religious questions from 45 BC onward, the research work of Varro and other contemporary antiquarians almost constitutes a science of Roman religion, which served as a source of reference on all matters concerning Roman religion right to the end of antiquity. A clear indication of this is the fact that considerable parts of Varro's *Divine Antiquities* are preserved thanks to the abundant quotations from it found in the writing of Augustine.

1.3 The place of myth

One has only to open the books written by the ancients or to contemplate the decoration of cult sites to see that mythological, historical and political 'commentaries' made their mark. The decorative scheme of the Forum of Augustus, surrounding the temple of Mars the Avenger, dedicated in 2 BC, clearly presented an image of civil war overcome and a Rome now reconciled, all thanks to Augustus. At the same time images were designed to cast Roman history since its Trojan origins as a history that led up to the Principate of Augustus. Countless temples in Rome and the rest of the Roman world received the same treatment. Their repertoire of sculpture and painting celebrated the person of the emperor and his family by associating them with the benefits and objectives of the cult.

Mythological interpretations of religious phenomena were legion. It was rare to find a cult site or even an altar or cult instruments that were not adorned with mythological scenes. It is likewise rare to find explanations of festivals and rites that are not based on mythical stories. It would, however, be mistaken to conclude that those myths belonged to Roman religion as a corpus of beliefs and certainties, with the same standing as revelation in the religions that stem from the Bible. The sources in fact show that myths were never used in the cult, except as an ornament designed to amuse the gods and afford them pleasure. Hymns, for example, were precious offerings, like any other consecrated work of art; they were not prayers. Neither the calendar nor the celebration of the Roman religion actualised or represented the unfolding of a myth as, for example, does Christianity.

In no sense did the myths constitute dogmas. What we understand by myth is a particular kind of story, or rather an aggregation of categories, which, when linked together, produces a story, an image or a ritual that expresses important data relating to the order of things: the birth of the world, of society and its institutions, the gods and relations with human beings, and so on. Traditionally, the tendency has been to separate Roman 'legends' from Greek myth, with the implicit suggestion that only classical and archaic Greece was 'mythopoietic', the Hellenistic and Roman periods being considered as an era of mythology and professors. However, it is clear that 'mythical thought' was still operational in the Hellenistic and Roman periods, at the very least because myths are always recreated each time they are told or represented visually. Added to this is the fact that myths do not have to be ancient, literally 'exact', non-contradictory and authentic to rate as 'myths'. Even in archaic and classical Greece, the 'great' myths were constantly re-elaborated to suit the context, and authenticity played no role at all. After all, myth transmits not truths or beliefs, but in the first instance statements of all kinds. In this area, as with other forms of interpretation, there is no dogma or rule apart from verisimilitude and the rules of the genre in which the statement is produced. The fact that Ovid and Plutarch frequently simultaneously put forward several myths reckoned to explain a festival, a ritual or some institution indicates that they had no intention of proposing the right interpretation. The reader was invited to accept all these myths at once, and to regard them as a series of statements, based on a ritual or institutional tradition, that might help him or her to progress beyond the surface of reality and explore its hidden background.

Myths take multiple forms, ranging from a great story to an etymological definition, and they adopt a variety of points of view, now historical and institutional, now grammatical or philosophical. Scholars frequently draw distinctions between these different types of myths, calling some aetiologies ('explanations of causes'), others myths. But, leaving literary qualitites aside, in truth there is no substantial difference between the various ways of giving expression to a myth. Sometimes, in etymology for example, the myth is reduced to a sort of 'degree zero'. Sometimes it is developed into a more or less long narrative. But the 'myth' itself, that aggregate of ideas that produces the statement, is present in all its versions.

In Rome, one of the most favoured forms of myth was history. It was treated in two different ways. In one, it is the city of Rome itself that provides the framework for the mythic story. In this context, the origin of things corresponded to the foundation of Rome, and the system of the world corresponded to the institutions of the *respublica*. In a sense, the history of the kings of Rome and some of the stories about the early Republic were in fact myths setting out the idea of the Roman city and constituting an ideal origin for the later evolution of Rome. Georges Dumézil has shown that the structure of these narratives matches closely that of myths (so favoured in certain other cultures) relating to the very beginning of time; and that this transposition to the early days of Rome in no way diminishes their mythic force. The Greeks too were familiar with aetiology and stories relating to the beginnings of their institutions. We should then resist the temptation to treat as 'history' what is actually an account of a perfect world-order or, in Roman terms, the ideal city.

The Romans also adopted the Greek mythical model when setting out their myths. Many of Ovid's myths, for example, are composed with the aid of Greek mythical themes familiar to everyone. In fact, in his *Fasti*, Ovid often gives first a 'Roman-style' account, then the 'Greek-style' one, and the structure of the myth and of its expression remains the same in both cases. This interlacing of myths was also designed to show that Roman culture is explained by that of the Greeks, and the destinies of the two cultures merge and complement each other. In this case, the mythical genre plays with the culture of its listeners to recreate a new myth, rather than invent a completely original story from scratch. But that diminishes neither the value nor the authenticity of the myths. As with etymologies and other types of exegesis, the accumulation of versions makes it possible to vary the scope of the statements in question and to introduce new nuances.

It is, of course, perfectly legitimate to raise the question of a myth's antiquity, particularly one that appears Roman or Italic. There exists no literature or other artistic oeuvre comparable to those of archaic and classical Greece, and most Roman myths are known in versions that date from the early Empire. In their desire to get back to Italic or Indo-European mythical themes, modern scholars have always tried to push that date back, postulating that the myths in question are far more ancient. Unfortunately, given the dearth of documents, most of those reconstructions remain hypothetical and, so far, only the comparative method of Georges Dumézil has succeeded in providing examples of Roman mythical themes that also exist in other cultures. But to compare is not to identify and, for historians, the problems are only just beginning when they detect a structural resemblance between two narratives.

1.4 The image

Images play a major role in the exegesis of cult. Recent works show that, from the second century BC on, the Roman elite set great store by the decoration of cult sites. Mythological imagery has already been mentioned; but it should be added that the implications of those images frequently went beyond the 'historical' or political level and made statements that were essentially philosophical. One of the first known examples of mythological imagery (referred to above in connection with calendars) was the scheme of the temple of Hercules and the Muses devised by Fulvius Nobilior, between 180 and 170 BC. In the colonnade surrounding this temple, Fulvius set up a calendar, preceded by a brief inscription on the origin of the names of the month. This calendar introduced a new way of representing the time of the year, by inscribing on the Fasti the anniversaries of the dedication of temples. It was a discreet way of writing the history of Rome and above all that of the victorious generals who had dedicated those buildings. We also know that the decorative programme of the temple of Hercules, perhaps inspired by the poet Ennius, associated it with Pythagoreanism and with King Numa. In this way, Fulvius proclaimed his own high culture as well as that of the Romans, which went back, through the time of Numa, all the way to Pythagoras, and which now laid down the law for the Greeks themselves: Hercules, the Pythagorean and civilising hero of the Romans, and also the protector of victorious Roman generals, was depicted playing a lyre (an allusion to the harmony of the spheres and so also to philosophy and knowledge of the cosmic order), standing before the choir of the Muses. When approaching the temple of Hercules and the Muses, built with the booty captured with Ambracia, the visitor or celebrant could not but be struck by the message of the decor and the inscriptions: this cult was designed to express Rome's domination over the Greeks, thanks to a general of Herculean invincibility and culture.

All Rome's major building programmes of the first century BC displayed representations of the order of things, including the place in that order of Rome's greatest men, Lutatius Catullus, Pompey and Caesar. But it was above all from the time of Augustus that this type of interpretation built into sacred places and cult sites became widespread, to the greater glory of the emperor. From then on, most cult sites were, if possible, enclosed in a rectangular colonnade that created visual axes that spelled out the message of the decor to whoever entered the temple or stood on its main axis. Whether that message was political or philosophical, or both at once, it always offered an additional commentary on the literal meaning of the cult.

2 THE PHILOSOPHY OF RELIGIONS

In their interpretations of cultural traditions, Varro and Cicero used, discussed and disseminated philosophical ideas. Cicero's treatises generally brought representatives of two or three different schools of thought together in debate, and on Cicero's own admission his books were designed to spread philosophical wisdom among his contemporaries. Nevertheless, the ultimate reference in these treatises was always the city, its ideals and its traditions. Varro writes explicitly as follows:

> If he were founding that city (Rome) anew, he would consecrate the gods and give them names according to the principles of nature (i.e. philosophy), rather than as they are now. But, as it is, since he is living in an old country, he says that he must keep the traditional account of the names and surnames (received from the ancients as that account was transmitted).
>
> Augustine, *City of God*, 4.31 = Varro,
> *Divine Antiquities*, fr. 12, ed. Cardauns

Alongside the 'civic' doctrine praised by the Roman theologians, there existed systems of a philosophical interpretation of religions. Although they were not entirely separate from the civic ideals, these systems, Greek in origin, pursued their own, different ends. They proposed very different interpretations of the gods and of religion. This is not the place to enter into a detailed discussion of the doctrines of the philosophical schools of the Roman period, for that is the subject of plenty of specialised works. A few general remarks will be sufficient on the theories with which all cultivated Romans must have been familiar. Obviously, to most Roman citizens, that is to say all those who were illiterate, these systems meant nothing at all. Philosophical allusions in the decorative schemes of temples and sanctuaries were far more likely to pass over their heads than political interpretations were.

During the second century BC the Romans had progressively encountered the ideas of the Greek philosophical schools. This foreign wisdom was still a subject of debate in the early second century, but little by little it came to constitute one of the bases of high Roman culture and, it follows, of Roman reflection upon the gods, religion and the

order of things; so much so that many Hellenistic philosophical traditions have been preserved for us and transmitted
by Roman sources. Of all the great schools of philosophy, it
was the Stoic system that dominated. Varro borrowed some
of his techniques of interpretation from the Stoics, in
particular the etymological method and allegorical exegesis.
A century later, Seneca too was inspired essentially by the
Stoic system. Lucretius, on the other hand, Varro's contemporary, referred back to the teaching of Epicurus, while
Cicero used all three of the major systems (Epicurean, Stoic
and Academic) at the same time – not that this was an innovation on his part, as by this time communication between
the schools had become commonplace. All these schools also
diffused Pythagorean ideas, which were spread most actively
by the Platonic school – from which the Pythagorean sects
derived.

All these philosophical interpretations of religion and the
gods, which are found in particular in the works of Varro and
Cicero, should be appreciated in their context. They constitute non-exclusive commentaries on the traditional religious
system, which they had no ambitions to replace. On the
contrary, even if they made philosophical wisdom the height
of all human aspirations, to explain the order of things philosophical interpretations themselves *used* religion, its rituals
and all that surrounded them. As an element in the working
of the world, that is to say as a collection of rules designed to
manage relations between any given community and the
gods, religious prescriptions were not meant to look 'behind'
things. Their job was to represent, and in a sense to create,
the reality of the present and visible world. Nevertheless, they
did establish a link with the immortal gods and they did go
back to a venerable period. So the various elements of religion, from the rituals themselves down to ritual instruments
and technical vocabulary, were all brought into play, along
with other Roman traditions, in speculation aiming to progress further in the exegesis and understanding of the visible
order. Thanks to learned methods refined by the Hellenistic

philosophical schools, scholars brought to light the hidden face of things and the ultimate reason for institutions, customs and even the deities.

Such interpretations flowered above all in philosophical treatises and poetry, and in glosses on the latter. But, as has been shown, they also inspired certain monuments and works of art. We have already mentioned the temple of Hercules and the Muses in this connection. Other examples are provided by Pompey's Theatre and the painted frescoes in certain villas of the Roman nobility around the bay of Naples. The implicit messages that these conveyed were almost a kind of game for the elite, who alone were capable of understanding the ultimate significance of particular architectural or decorative details (for example, a sphere). With a wink or nudge of this sort, the artist proposed an interpretation of religious institutions, history or reality that represented the world and its order in philosophical terms that matched up to the aspirations of the cultivated elite.

It is, however, worth noting that, in the domain of interpretation and speculation, the same rules applied as in religious life itself: there was no absolute dogma or authority to impose the 'right' interpretation. One proposition was as good as another; they were all juxtaposed, and their relevance was judged by philosophical rules rather than in relation to religion. Of course, philosophical explanations did not take the place of religious practice, in the strict sense of the expression, at least not among the philosophers of the end of the Republican era and the first century of the Empire. Like those of the antiquarians, their interpretations were not intended to break away from religious traditions. However, from the third century onward, the Neo-Platonists did progressively do so, detaching themselves more and more from the ideal of the city and the traditional religion. Those who defended traditional religion in the fourth century tended to associate religious practice with a basis of beliefs of a philosophical nature or even with mystical practices (Plotinus), which fundamentally differed very little from Christianity. By this time, the religion inspired by the model of the city had run out of steam, chiefly as a result of the disasters that had befallen the Empire since the mid-third century. And, as tended to happen in this type of religion, the Romans had given up on some of their gods and above all on a particular kind of relationship with them. The distant relations between mortals and immortals characteristic of the civic model, relations which respected liberty, were gradually replaced by much closer links with the gods, which the ancestors of the fourth-century Romans would have described as 'super-stitious'. The new piety greatly stressed human inferiority and submission to the gods, underlining the importance of knowledge of what happened *beyond* this world rather than efforts to establish and maintain good relations with the immortals *within* it and with a view to life in the here and now.

3 MYSTERY CULTS

Scholars for a long time contrasted Roman traditions with what they called the 'Eastern cults' or 'mystery cults', fre-quently assimilating the two. As we have noted above, it was from this type of cult that the religious evolution leading to the Christian religions was supposed to have developed. The Romans were even supposed to have been gradually aban-doning their own ritualistic traditions and turning to these 'new' religions ever since the second century BC. It is an unconvincing theory (see above, Chapter 1) and we need not dwell on it here – except (following Walter Burkert, whose work is summarised below) briefly to correct some of the basic inaccuracies in modern accounts of the mystery cults.

Contrary to what is still often believed, the mystery cults were not a late and new phenomenon, for they had existed in Greece ever since the sixth century BC. Although they may have been grafted on to cults of an Eastern origin, they were not themselves 'Eastern cults', but stemmed above all from Eleusis and the cult of Dionysus. Nor were the mystery cults religions of salvation and spirituality. In the first place, they constituted not religions, but 'variable forms, tendencies and options within the sole conglomerate . . . of ancient religion'. The wellbeing or salvation sought by these cults was of a nature just as material as that offered by the traditional cults: it had to do with this world, with the here and now. True, they showed that death was not an evil, and offered hope for the beyond, but above all they set out to achieve a happy life in this world and possibly even to prolong it and help the deceased after their deaths. Initiates basically sought a particular intimacy with one or several deities who were supposed to ensure their wellbeing, in life as in death, rather than to become initiated into a systematic theology that was oriented towards salvation for the soul. Fundamentally, these experiences differed from the rites of magic or theurgy only in their communal character and the fact that they were directed towards the good, whereas the intimacy with a deity (of the world below) sought by the men and women who practised rites of sorcery were often designed to do harm. But in principle, a sorceror sought a personal encounter with a deity, as did those initiated into mystery cults or, from the second century AD, into certain gnostic and philosophical movements. The only difference was that the sorceror did this through prescribed rites to discover secrets and acquire some power over the deity in question – but not in order to gain union with that deity. Far more than the mysteries and, of course, certain rites of sorcery, the Neo-Platonists, for their part, cultivated asceticism, spirituality, and the mystic experience to be obtained by momentarily separating the soul from the body. The founder of Neo-Platonism, Plotinus (c.205–70), was reputed to have achieved that experience four times in his life.

Mystery cults changed an individual's relationship with the deity in the present world by means of rituals of initiation and purification. But (except in Mithraism, in which there were different hierarchical grades) those initiations did not represent a visible or definitive change of state for an individual. These cults were practised alongside the other city cults.

Furthermore, plenty of 'mystic' rites were accomplished in order to fulfil vows whose objective was entirely material. As Walter Burkert explains, this was an experimental form of religion, which sought out the most efficacious deities and tried to win their friendship. There is no similarity between these cults and Christianity. They conveyed no message of triumph over death nor did they offer any fundamentally new revelations. The only document that provides direct information on Mithraic initiation, a tiny fragment of a fourth-century 'catechism' recently published by William Brashear, offers us nothing but an exchange of coded questions and answers between an initiate and a cult dignitary, an exchange that contains no consistent information on the doctrine of this cult and is mainly concerned with the ritual aspects of initiation. The cult of the Great Mother was also progressively associated with mysteries, explicitly mentioned only in the fourth century AD, but detectable as early as the second century. Through a sacrifice (for the wellbeing of the emperor) of a bull or a ram, the testicles of which were offered to the Mother as a substitute for self-mutilation, the celebrants could consecrate themselves to the goddess by a ritual similar to that practised by the *galli*. In gnostic texts, the philosophical exegesis of these practices is more explicit. The Naassenes offered a spiritual interpretation of the Anatolian myth and rites of the Great Mother. The castration of Attis represented the soul's ascent into the upper, eternal sphere, where the distinction between the sexes no longer existed. The new being thus created was at once both male and female. This exegesis may give some idea of the interpretations produced by mystic groups.

4 NEIGHBOURING RELIGIONS

The mysteries do not altogether correspond to the religious change postulated by some historians in the past. What they really constituted was a particular manifestation of ritualism at the interface of ritual tradition and philosophy. From this point of view, the Romans' day-to-day contact with 'truly' Eastern religions, Judaism, and Christian and Gnostic movements, certainly made a more profound impression on the evolution of traditional religion than did the mystery cults, which were always a limited phenomenon.

In Rome and in all the cities of the Empire, many religious systems rubbed shoulders. They were sometimes quite different in their representation of the deity, in the religious roles they offered to individuals and the final objective of their piety. Jewish communities had been established in Rome ever since the second century BC and, despite the terrible upheaval of revolts in the first and second centuries AD, they continued to flourish throughout the Empire, both in Rome and elsewhere. Christian communities, which were distinguished hardly at all from the Jews until the second century, were also firmly planted in towns throughout the Empire. Despite the persecutions that struck them from time to time, particularly from the mid-third century on, long periods of relative calm allowed them to practise their religion freely, so long as it gave rise to no public disturbances. That liberty was even greater at the domestic level.

Inevitably, therefore, Romans were progressively initiated, more or less, into religions different from their own. And indeed it has been shown that the boundaries between all these communities and the Romans who practised their traditional religion were by no means as firm as has sometimes been believed. Everything led to such contacts. The Romans should not be imagined as unshakeably faithful to one particular religion. In the first place, they belonged not to a single religion but to several: that of the family, that of the city district, etc. Moreover, accustomed as they were to practising whatever kind of cult suited the social situation, the Romans were not tied to a single form of 'belief'. Most of their traditional religious systems involved no formal initiation and so easily accepted the participation of neighbours and strangers. So, it is not surprising to find Romans switching from one type of cult to another, depending on where they were or what they were engaged in (trade, a particular profession, navigation). They would on occasion participate in a ritual banquet with Jewish partners or neighbours. Inscriptions also testify to the existence of Roman 'god fearers' (not Jews but in the penumbra of Judaism) among the benefactors of synagogues. Yet others, who up until the second century seemed to be Jews, were spreading a different kind of word that the Romans gradually began to hear. One of Augustine's sermons dating from the beginning of the year 404 was adressed directly to 'pagans', which shows that these would attend sermons among the Christians, only leaving the church at the moment of the eucharistic office. Treatises in defence of Christianity ('apologetic treatises') also sought to diffuse Christian teaching among 'pagans', whether sympathisers or not. Conversely, some Jewish or Christian neighbours would take part in family or local city festivals, not to mention the great sacrificial banquets and public Games. The Church Fathers' disapproval of such religious promiscuity is vigorous enough to suggest that the behaviour was common.

However, comparisons were gradually made, and new religious forms developed. It is reasonable to suppose that the later versions of mystery cults were a product of the mixing of religious communities. The long pre-eminence of traditional ritualism over the preceding centuries does not rule out the existence of a kind of religiosity founded upon the perfecting of an individual's personality and a quest for salvation for the soul. The only difference from later religions was the different balance maintained between spirituality and ritualism. Thus, the progressive interest shown in a type of religious experience that aimed for contact between the human soul and the deity did not necessarily constitute a spiritual revolution, but rather involved a shifting of the balance between religious notions stimulated by a philosophical education and above all by the new religions. Some 'pagans' stressed the initiatory and mystical aspect of the traditional religion. Sometimes they did this by means of an allegorical interpretation, like the one penned by Emperor Julian, sometimes by citing a vast accumulation of initiations associated with all the mysteries of the Roman world, as in the circle of Vettius Agorius Praetextatus. But these phenomena date from the fourth century AD, by which time the city ideal, as such, had faded away and the misfortunes of the times had caused many Romans to doubt the protection said to be afforded by the traditional gods. Instances of the survival of traditional practices chiefly involved the aristocracy, which preserved a selection of public cults, now celebrated as domestic ones, by transforming them into a kind of philoso-phising religion. But a series of laws prohibiting the practice of traditional rites eventually transposed the problem to a different level. Conversion now concentrated upon purging Christian practices of the kind of automatic assumptions and responses that went along with Graeco-Roman ritualism.

Chronology

Dates	Historical events	Religious events
754 BC	Legendary date of the foundation of Rome.	
754–509 BC	**The Regal period** (Rome ruled by kings).	
509–27 BC	**The Republic.**	
13 Sept. 509 BC		Traditional date of the dedication of the temple of Capitoline Jupiter.
17 Dec. 497 BC		Traditional date of the dedication of the temple of Saturn.
19 April 493 BC		Traditional date of the dedication of the temple of Ceres, Liber and Libera, on the Aventine.
27 Jan. 484 BC		Traditional date of the consecration of the temple of Castor in the Forum.
451–450 BC	The Laws of the Twelve Tables.	
13 July(?) 431 BC		Traditional date of the dedication of the temple of Apollo (close to the later Theatre of Marcellus).

Dates	Historical events	Religious events
399 BC		First celebration of a *lectisternium* organised by the *duouiri sacris faciundis*.
390 BC	Sack of Rome by the Gauls.	Foundation of a temple to Aius Locutius.
367 BC	The Licinian Laws, opening the Consulate to the *plebs*.	Plebeians become *decemuiri sacris faciundis*.
366 BC		The Roman Games (4–17 Sept., banquet of Jupiter 13 Sept.) become an annual festival.
340 BC	War against the Latins.	(Legendary?) devotion of the Consul Publius Decius Mus in the battle close to the Veseris, in Campania.
312 BC	Censorship of Appius Claudius. Construction of the Appian Way and the first aqueduct.	The cult of Hercules of the Great Altar (Forum Boarium), traditionally officiated by the Potitii, is taken over by the state and committed to the care of public slaves.

Dates	Historical events	Religious events
304 BC	The scribe Cnaeus Flavius marks the dates of *dies fasti* and *nefasti* on the calendar.	The creation of the parade of Roman knights (*transuectio equitum*) from the temple of Mars to the Capena Gate and the temple of Castor (15 July).
300 BC		The *Lex Ogulnia* allows plebeians to enter the College of Pontiffs and the College of Augurs; the number of priests in public colleges is increased.
295 BC	Second Samnite War (298–291 BC).	Devotion of Publius Decius Mus (son of the elder Publius Decius Mus) in the Battle of Sentinum.
293 BC		Introduction of the cult of Aesculapius on the recommendation of the Sibylline Books (dedication of the temple of Aesculapius on the Tiber Island, on 1 Jan. 291 BC).
287 BC	The *Lex Hortensia* marks the end of the struggle between the orders.	

Dates	Historical events	Religious events
272–264 BC	Rome completes the conquest of Italy.	
264–241 BC	First Punic War.	
254–244 BC		First plebeian *pontifex maximus* (Tiberius Coruncanius).
228 BC		Two couples (one Greek, one Gallic) buried alive in the Forum Boarium.
221 BC	Hannibal becomes leader of the Carthaginian army. Creation of the Circus Flaminius.	
220 BC		The Plebeian Games (4–17 Nov., banquet of Jupiter 13 Nov.) become annual.
218–202 BC	Second Punic War.	
217 BC	Start of Second Punic War. Hannibal crosses the Alps.	Many prodigies: the Sibylline Books are consulted, and expiatory ceremonies are held.
216 BC	Hannibal crushes the Romans at Cannae.	Two couples (one Greek, one Gallic) buried alive in the Forum Boarium.

Dates	Historical events	Religious events
215 BC		The *Lex Sempronia* rules that public temples must be dedicated by two specially elected men (*duumuiri aedi dedicandae*).
213 BC	Hannibal takes Tarentum.	Panic in Rome. Measures taken against superstition. The *carmine Marciana* (prophecies of the Marcius brothers) are added to the Sibylline Books.
212 BC		From now on, the *pontifex maximus* is elected by the *comitia tributa*. Institution of the Games of Apollo.
211 BC	Hannibal marches on Rome.	
207 BC		Many prodigies, one being the extinction of the flame of Vesta.
205 BC		Introduction of the Great Mother (Cybele) to Rome, on the advice of the Sibylline Books, in order to win victory.

Dates	Historical events	Religious events
4 April 204 BC	Scipio goes to Africa.	The Great Mother is welcomed to Rome and installed in the temple of Victory (Palatine). Creation of the *Ludi Megalenses* (Games of the Great Mother).
202 BC	Roman victory at Zama.	
200–197 BC	Macedonian War.	
197–181 BC	Submission of Cisalpine Gaul (Po Valley).	
196 BC		The *Lex Licinia* creates three *epulones*, responsible for sacred banquets.
195 BC		The *uer sacrum*, vowed in 217 BC, is carried out. This is repeated in 194 BC because of a formal irregularity.
191 BC	The *Lex Acilia* entrusts intercalation to the pontiffs.	Dedication of the temple of the Great Mother on the Palatine. The fast of Ceres (*ieiunium Cereris*) becomes annual and official.

Dates	Historical events	Religious events
30 June 189 BC		Fulvius Nobilior vows a temple to Hercules 'of the Muses', completed between 180 and 170 BC.
186 BC		Scandal of the Bacchanalia and repression.
181 BC		Discovery on the Janiculan, in a tomb, and destruction of the books 'of Numa' (claimed to be Pythagorean).
175 BC	Expulsion of the Epicurean philosophers Alcaeus and Philiscos(?).	
173 BC	Expulsion of philosophers.	The Games of Flora become annual.
156–155 BC	Embassy of the philosophers Diogenes, Critolaos and Carneades.	
154 BC	The *Leges Aelia* and *Fufia* rule that magistrates have the right to challenge the lawfulness of *comitia* by announcing unfavourable signs (*obnuntiatio*).	

Dates	Historical events	Religious events
153 BC	The start of the civic year is fixed to 1 Jan. (when consuls take up their duties).	
149–146 BC	Third Punic War.	
146 BC	Destruction of Carthage. Expulsion of the Chaldaeans (astrologers).	Evocation of the gods of Carthage.
133 BC	Tiberius Gracchus tribune of the *plebs*.	
132 BC	Tiberius Gracchus assassinated.	
123–122 BC	Gaius Gracchus tribune of the *plebs*.	
121 BC	Assassination of Gaius Gracchus.	
114 BC		Two couples (one Greek, one Gallic) buried alive in the Forum Boarium.
104–103 BC		The *Lex Domitia* entrusts the election of priests to the four major colleges to the *comitia tributa*.
91–88 BC	Social War.	
89–82 BC		Quintus Mucius Scaevola becomes *pontifex maximus*.

Dates	Historical events	Religious events
87–80 BC	Civil War between the supporters of Marius and the Julia.	
87 BC	Rome taken by Marius and Cinna.	Suicide of the *flamen* of Jupiter Cornelius Merula. This flaminate then remains vacant until 11 BC.
83 BC		The Capitol fire and the destruction of the Sibylline Books.
82 BC	Sylla's dictatorship. The Sullan Laws.	Assassination of the *pontifex maximus* Quintus Mucius Scaevola in the Sanctuary of Vesta; the *Lex Cornelia* on priesthoods repeals the *Lex Domitia* and increases the number of priests.
76 BC		Reconstitution of the Sibylline Books.
69 BC		Dedication of the new Capitoline temple.
65 BC		The *Lex Papia* on the election of the Vestals, limiting the powers of the *pontifex maximus.*

Dates	Historical events	Religious events
63 BC	Consulate of Cicero. Conspiracy of Catilina.	The *Lex Atia* on priesthoods repeals the *Lex Cornelia* and returns to the provisions of the *Lex Domitia*; Julius Caesar is elected *pontifex maximus*.
62 BC		The Bona Dea affair (Clodius, disguised as a woman, defiles the mysteries of Bona Dea).
59 BC	Consulate of Caesar.	Destruction of the altars of Isis and Serapis on the Capitol.
58 BC	Caesar in Gaul (58–51 BC).	A law of Clodius, tribune of the *plebs*, limits the right of *obnuntiatio*.
50–48 BC	Civil War between Caesar and Pompey.	
49–46 BC		The *Lex Iulia* on priests.
46 BC	Caesar's reform of the calendar.	
44 BC	Assassination of Caesar. The name of the month Quintilis is changed to Iulius.	Lepidus becomes *pontifex maximus*.
43 BC	Octavian for the first time receives *imperium*.	

Dates	Historical events	Religious events
42 BC	Battle of Philippi.	Deification of Caesar by the *Lex Rufrena*.
36 BC		Octavian's vow regarding the temple of Apollo Palatine.
33 BC	Expulsions of Chaldeans.	
32 BC	Octavian declares war on Egypt following the ritual of the *fetiales*.	
31 BC	The victory of Actium.	
1 Aug. 30 BC	Capture of Alexandria. Octavian sole master of the Empire; end of the Civil War.	
18 Aug. 29 BC		Dedication of the temple of the *diuus Iulius* (the deified Julius).
27 BC–AD 476	**The Empire**	
27 BC –AD 68	The Julio-Claudian dynasty	
13 Jan. 27 BC	Octavian is named Augustus.	Programme for the restoration of cults and sacred buildings.

Dates	Historical events	Religious events
9 Oct. 28 BC		Dedication of the temple of Apollo Palatine.
28 BC		Shrines of Isis banned within the pomerium. Restoration of the Arval Brethren(?). Four-yearly Games for the wellbeing of Augustus.
27–25 BC		Agrippa has the Pantheon built.
17 BC		Fifth Secular Games.
6 March 12 BC		Augustus elected *pontifex maximus*.
28 April 12 BC		Dedication of an altar to Vesta in Augustus' house on the Palatine.
From 12 BC on		Reconstitution of the colleges celebrating the cult of the Lares of the crossroads and the Games at the Compitalia.
11 BC		The *flamen* of Jupiter is appointed again.
30 Jan. 9 BC		Dedication of the altar of the Ara Pacis Augustae.

Dates	Historical events	Religious events
8 BC	The month Sextilis is renamed Augustus. Last correction to Caesar's calendar reform.	
2 BC		Augustus is named *pater patriae* by the Senate. Dedication of the temple of Mars Ultor in the Forum of Augustus.
14	Death of Augustus. Tiberius becomes emperor.	Deification of Augustus. Creation of *sodales Augustales* and a *flamen Augustalis* to celebrate his cult.
19		Following a scandal, Tiberius has the Iseum destroyed and the statue of Isis cast into the Tiber.
37	Death of Tiberius. Caligula becomes emperor.	Dedication of the temple of the *diuus Augustus* on the Palatine.
38		Caligula has a temple for Isis built on the Campus Martius.
41	Assassination of Caligula. Claudius becomes emperor.	

Dates	Historical events	Religious events
41/54		Public recognition of the 'Phrygian' festival of the Great Mother in March; authorisation for the college of *dendrophori*.
42		Deification of Livia (*diua Augusta*).
48		Secular Games on the occasion of the eighth centenary of the foundation of Rome.
54	Death of Claudius. Nero becomes emperor.	Claudius is deified.
64	The fire of Rome. Persecution of Christians.	Dedication of the temple of the *diuus Claudius* on the Caelian.
68–9	Assassination of Nero. Civil War. The Capitol fire.	
70–96	The Flavian dynasty	
70	Vespasian emperor. Destruction of the town and temple of Jerusalem by Titus.	

Dates	Historical events	Religious events
Last quarter of the first century AD		The cult of Mithras is established in Rome and Italy.
79–81	Death of Vespasian. Titus emperor. Death of Titus. Domitian emperor.	Deification of Vespasian and Titus.
86		Creation of the Capitoline *Agon* in honour of the Capitoline Triad.
88		Sixth Secular Games.
96–192	The Antonine dynasty	
96	Assassination of Domitian. Nerva emperor.	
98	Death of Nerva. Trajan emperor.	Deification of Nerva.
117	Death of Trajan. Hadrian emperor.	Deification of Trajan.
118–19		Reconstruction of Pantheon. Dedication of the temple of the *diuus Trajan* in the Forum of Trajan.
132–5	Second Jewish War. A Roman colony installed in Jerusalem.	

Dates	Historical events	Religious events
135		Dedication of the temple of Venus and Rome on the Sacra Via.
138	Death of Hadrian. Antoninus emperor.	Deification of Hadrian.
141		Dedication of the temple of the *diua Faustina* (later also of the *diuus Antoninus*).
145		Dedication of the temple of the *diuus Hadrian* on the Campus Martius.
148		Secular Games to celebrate the ninth centenary of the foundation of Rome.
From the mid-second century AD on		The cult of Mithras is established in the provinces. The *taurobolium* is now part of the cult of the Great Mother.
161	Death of Antoninus. Marcus Aurelius and Lucius Verus emperors.	Deification of Antoninus.
169	Death of Lucius Verus.	Deification of Lucius Verus.
180	Death of Marcus Aurelius. Commodus emperor.	Deification of Marcus Aurelius.

Dates	Historical events	Religious events
193	Assassination of Commodus. Civil War (193–7).	
193–235	The Severan dynasty	
193–235	Septimius Severus proclaimed emperor.	Deification of Commodus.
197	*Apologeticus* of Tertullian.	
202	Edict prohibiting Jewish and Christian proselytism. Persecution of Christians.	
204		Seventh Secular Games.
211	Death of Septimus Severus. Caracalla and Geta emperors.	Deification of Septimus Severus.
212	Edict of Caracalla granting Roman citizenship to all free *peregrini*. Assassination of Geta.	
217	Assassination of Caracalla. Elagabalus emperor.	Deification of Caracalla.
217–22		Elagabalus introduces the cult of the sun god Elagabalus.

Dates	Historical events	Religious events
222	Elagabalus assassinated. Severus Alexander emperor.	
235–85	Crisis and disturbances	
248	Philip the Arab emperor (244–9).	Secular Games celebrating the millennium of the foundation of Rome.
250	Trajan Decius emperor (249–51). Persecution of Christians.	Edict of Decius obliging citizens to sacrifice to the gods.
257		Edict of Valerian (253–60) banning the Christian cult.
260	Valerian captured by the king of the Persians. Reforms of Gallienus (253–68).	A return to tolerance of the Christians.
274	Aurelian emperor (270–5).	Dedication of the temple of Sol Invictus.
284	Advent of Diocletian (284–305).	
286	Maximian proclaimed Augustus (284–305).	
293	Constantius and Galerus declared Caesars.	
293–305	The Tetrarchy	

Dates	Historical events	Religious events
303–5		Major persecution under Diocletian.
305	Abdication of Diocletian and Maximian.	
306	Death of Constantius, usurpation of Constantine and Maxentius.	
311	Death of Galerius.	Edict of tolerance by Galerius recognising Christianity as an allowable religion.
312	Defeat of Maxentius. Constantine master of the West.	
312–83	Constantinian Empire	
313		'Edict of Milan': Christians granted freedom of worship, restitution of churches.
330	Foundation of Constantinople.	
331		Inventory of the possessions of temples.
337		Baptism of Constantine.
342		Imperial ruling bans sacrifices.

Dates	Historical events	Religious events
357–400		Dispute over the Altar of Victory (Symmachus).
361–3	Reign of Julian.	Pagan reaction.
367–83	Reign of Gratian.	
367		Restoration of the colonnade of the *dii consentes* close to the Roman Forum by Praetextatus.
378–95	Reign of Theodosius.	
379		Gratian refuses to wear the cloak of the *pontifex maximus*.
382		Measures taken by Gratian against paganism.
391		The Laws of Theodosius definitively ban pagan cult. Temples are closed and destroyed.
Soon after 400		Stilicho burns the Sibylline Books.
410	Sack of Rome by Alaric.	
494		Pope Gelasius I forbids the Christians of Rome to take part in the Lupercalia.

Principal people

Augustine (AD 354–430): Bishop of Hippo, Church Father. His *City of God* (written 413–26) is a very important source for the history of Roman religion.

Augustus (63 BC–AD 14): Caesar's adopted son. After defeating Mark Antony, he became the first Roman emperor.

Caligula (AD 12–41): Third Roman emperor.

Cato (234–149 BC): Roman senator. The author of, among other works, a treatise *On Agriculture*.

Cicero (106–43 BC): Roman senator. His literary oeuvre is one of the most important to have been preserved. It includes private correspondence and philosophical treatises, among many other kinds of writing.

Decii: A family two or three of whose members won fame by 'devoting' themselves to the gods of the underworld in battles in the fourth and third centuries BC.

Dionysius of Halicarnassus (late first century AD): Greek critic and historian. In the reign of Augustus he wrote a history of Rome in Greek (the surviving part covers the origins of the city down to the mid-fifth century BC).

Eudoxus of Cnidus (c.390–340 BC): Greek astronomer, mathematician and geographer.

Festus (second century AD): A Roman grammarian who summarised the dictionary of Verrius Flaccus entitled *On the Meaning of Words*, composed during the reign of Augustus.

Fulvius Nobilior (late third/early second century AD): Consul in 189 BC, and victor over the Aetolians. A cultivated man, associated with the poet Ennius. With the booty from his campaign, he built the temple of Hercules and the Muses in the Circus Flaminius.

Gaius (second century AD): Legal writer.

Germanicus (15 BC–AD 19): Adopted son of Emperor Tiberius, and his designated successor.

Gracchi: Roman senators, the brothers Tiberius (died 133 BC) and Gaius (died 121 BC). Both introduced radical 'popular' legislation and were killed in the political conflicts that followed.

Julian (AD 331–63): Roman emperor and strong supporter of pagan religion.

Julius Caesar (100–44 BC): Roman senator who, as 'dictator', effectively established one-man rule at Rome in the midfirst century BC. He was *pontifex maximus* from 63 BC until his assassination in 44.

Livy (59 BC–AD 17): Author of a Roman history in 142 books, covering the origins of Rome down to the Principate of Augustus. Only 35 books and a summary have survived.

Macrobius (early fifth century AD): Author of the *Saturnalia*, an encyclopedia written in the form of a literary banquet, which contains much information about religion.

Ovid (43 BC–AD 17): Roman poet whose works include a poem on the Roman calendar (*Fasti*) and many versions of Graeco-Roman myth

Paul Diaconus ('the deacon') (c.AD 730–79): A scholar of the Carolingian period and the author of, among other works, an abridged version of Festus' *On the Meaning of Words*.

Pliny the Elder (AD 23/4–79): Roman polymath and author of a multi-volume encyclopedia, the *Natural History*.

Pliny the Younger (c. AD 61–112): Roman senator and nephew of the elder Pliny. Author of a published collection of *Letters*.

Plutarch (late first/early second century AD): Prolific Greek writer and priest at the sanctuary of Apollo at Delphi. Numerous of his biographies, philosophical and antiquarian works survive.

Seneca (AD 1–65): Roman senator, consul (in 56) and Stoic philosopher. The tutor of Nero; very influential during the early years of Nero's Principate. Author of philosophical treatises and letters, and also tragedies.

Servius (late fourth/early fifth century AD): Grammarian and the author of a large commentary on the works of Virgil, which contains much information on religion.

Suetonius (late first/early second century AD): Roman equestrian who filled various posts in the imperial administration. Author of a surviving series of biographies of emperors.

Tacitus (c.AD 56–c.120): Roman senator (consul in 97) who wrote histories of the early empire (*Annals* and *Histories*).

Tertullian (c.AD 160–after 220): A Christian and the author of an *Apologeticus* (a defence of Christianity) who lived in Carthage.

Tiberius (42 BC–AD 37): Adopted son of Augustus, second Roman emperor.

Timaeus (c.350–260 BC): Greek historian from Sicily, whose works included a history of Rome's wars against King Pyrrhus in the early third century BC.

Valerius Maximus (first century AD): Author of a book of *Memorable Deeds and Sayings*, recording many anecdotes from the history of the Republic.

Varro (116–27 BC): Roman senator who, after a political career alongside Pompey, devoted himself to research and literary activities. In 47 he dedicated his *Divine Antiquities* to the *pontifex maximus*, Julius Caesar. Between 46 and his death, he published numerous works on literary and linguistic subjects.

Verrius Flaccus (c.55 BC–c.AD 20): Roman freedman and leading scholar of Latin and of Roman institutions. His lost work *On the Meaning of Words* is partly preserved in the summary of Festus.

Glossary

This gives technical terms in the study of Roman politics, culture and history.

antiquarians: Roman scholars who collected and studied ancient institutions, customs and linguistic forms.

bulla: Amulet worn by Roman children.

city: Political unit comprising a town and its territory.

client: A person, group or even city linked to a patron and protected by him. Clients would support their patron in return.

colony: A city outside Rome which operated in accordance with Roman law and normally populated by Roman citizens (but see 'Latin right' below). Colonies were in many cases founded to accommodate veteran soldiers or the Roman poor, but the title of colony could also be given as an honour to towns in the provinces.

comitia: Assemblies of the Roman people for legislation and elections. There were two main types: the *comitia centuriata* (which voted in groups known as 'centuries') and the *comitia tributa* (which voted in 'tribes').

decemuiri: Group of 'ten men' who ruled Rome as an emergency measure after civil conflict in the fifth century BC (not to be confused with the priesthood of the *decemuiri* (later *quindecemuiri*) *sacris faciundis* (see p. 136).

decurion: Member of the town council of a *municipium*.

duumuir (pl. *duouiri*): The two supreme magistrates in Roman towns and colonies.

Empire: The period of Roman history when Rome was ruled by an emperor, traditionally defined as 27 BC to AD 476.

freedman: A former slave.

gens: A Roman family or 'clan'.

Ides: The 'peak' of a month in the Roman calendar. They fell on either the 13th or the 15th of the month.

imperium: 'The power of supreme command' possessed by consuls and praetors. The terms 'empire' and 'emperor' are derivatives.

Indo-Europeans: Societies speaking one of the languages of the Indo-European group, attested from India to Gaul.

Kalends: The first day of the month in the Roman calendar.

lararium: Domestic shrine that housed representations of the Lares and the *genius* of the head of the family.

Latin right: The body of rights, originally granted to Rome's Italian neighbours, which included marriage, the bequeathing of possessions, and the right to occupy a magistracy and thereby become a Roman citizen. In so-called Latin colonies the inhabitants had the Latin right.

magistrate: An elected official who held power in the city. In Rome the principal magistrates were consuls, praetors, aediles, quaestors and tribunes of the *plebs*. In municipia and colonies they were *duouiri*, aediles and quaestors.

matron (Latin *matrona*): Married woman.

municipium (pl. *municipia*): A town in Italy or the provinces with some form of Roman status (normally, either full citizenship or the Latin right) and its own autonomous organisation.

Nones: In the Roman calendar, the 5th or the 7th of the month.

orthopraxis: A religious system founded on rites and their correct execution.

patrician: A legal term designating the descendants of families that belonged to the aristocracy at the beginning of the fifth century.

patron (Latin, *patronus*): A rich and influential citizen who protected clients (see above), who, in return, gave him their support in public life.

peregrini: A legal term designating foreigners who did not possess the rights of a Roman citizen or full Latin rights. There were also *peregrini* cities and peoples.

plebeian: A Roman citizen who was not a member of a patrician family.

'primitivists': Also known as 'predeists'. Historians (notably H. J. Rose and Ludwig Deubner) who identified the earliest phase of Roman religion with a stage prior to the invention of anthropomorphic gods. During this phase, it was suggested, deities were imagined as impersonal, vague, 'numinous' powers.

Principate: The political regime of the first two centuries or so of the Empire; used to distinguish this period from the increasingly autocratic conventions of the 'late Empire'.

Republic: The period extending from the traditional date of the foundation of the Republican regime in Rome, in 504 BC, to the beginning of the Principate, in 27 BC.

Senate: The council of Rome, made up of former magistrates.

sportula: A gift given by a patron to his clients.

suouetaurilia: A sacrifice to Mars consisting of a boar (*sus*), a ram (*ouis*) and a bull (*taurus*).

toga praetexta: A toga adorned with wide bands of purple. Reserved for magistrates and priests.

triclinium: Dining room or banquet hall.

triumphator: Victorious Roman general as he appeared in his triumph (or victory parade).

uicus: Either a small settlement situated in a city's territory and subordinated to that city, or the name given to the sub-district of a main town.

Further reading

TEXTS CITED

As far as possible, quotations from ancient authors are taken from the Loeb Classical Library (Harvard University Press), sometimes adapted.

Passages from Festus or Paul Diaconus are taken from the text of W. W. Lindsay, Sex. Pompeius Festus, *De verborum significatione* (Leipzig, 1913).

Inscriptions are cited from:

CIL   *Corpus Inscriptionum Latinarum* (Berlin, 1863)
ILLRP   A. Degrassi (ed.), *Inscriptiones Latinae Liberae Rei Publicae* (Florence, 1963)
ILS   H. Dessau (ed.) *Inscriptiones Latinae Selectae* (Berlin, 1892–1916)

GENERAL STUDIES

Classic works of reference

Latte, K. *Römische Religionsgeschichte* (Munich, 1960) – though see Brelich, A. 'Un libro dannoso', *Studi e Materiali di Storia delle Religioni* 32 (1961), 310–54

Wissowa, G. *Religion und Kultus der Römer* (2nd edn, Munich, 1912)

Recent works of reference and broad studies

Bayet, J. *Histoire politique et psychologique de la religion romaine* (Paris, 1969)

Beard, M., North, J., Price, S. *Religions of Rome* (Cambridge, 1998)

Dumézil, G. *Archaic Roman Religion* (Chicago, 1970)

Feeney, D. *Literature and Religion at Rome* (Cambridge, 1998)

Le Glay, M. *La religion romaine* (Paris, 1991)

Liebeschuetz, J. H. W. G. *Continuity and Change in Roman Religion* (Oxford, 1979)

Rüpke, J. *Domi militiae. Die religiöse Konstruktion des Krieges in Rom* (Stuttgart, 1990)

Scheid, J. *Religion et piété à Rome* (Paris, 1985; 2nd edn 2001)

Encyclopaedias

Le Grand Atlas des religions. Encyclopaedia Universalis (Paris, 1988)

Johnston, S. Iles (ed.), *Religions of the Ancient World* (Cambridge, MA, forthcoming)

Aufstieg und Niedergang der römischen Welt (Berlin & New York). This encyclopaedia contains essays on many topics – of varying quality. See especially volumes II, 16 & 17 (Rome and Italy), 18 (provinces), 19–21 (Judaism), 22 (gnosticism), 23ff (Christianity)

Important essays and collections

Ando, C. (ed.) *Roman Religion. Edinburgh Readings on the Ancient World* (Edinburgh, 2003)

Gordon, R. 'From Republic to Principate', 'The Veil of Power' and 'Religion in the Roman Empire' in M. Beard and J. North (eds), *Pagan Priests* (London, 1990)

Momigliano, A. *On Pagans, Jews and Christians* (Middletown, Connecticut, 1987)

Nock, A. D. *Essays on Religion and the Ancient World* (Oxford, 1972)

North, J. 'Conservatism and Change in Roman Religion', *PBSR* 44 (1976), 1–12

STUDIES OF PARTICULAR ASPECTS

Magic

Graf, F. *Magic in the Ancient World* (Cambridge, MA, 1997)

Republic and before

Bispham, E. and C. Smith (eds), *Religion in Archaic and Republican Rome and Italy* (Edinburgh, 2000)

Cornell, T. J. *The Beginnings of Rome. Italy and Rome from the Bronze Age to the Punic Wars (c. 1000 BC–264 BC)* (London & New York, 1995)

Momigliano. A. 'The Origins of Rome' in *Cambridge Ancient History*, VII (Cambridge, 1989), 52–112

Pailler, J.-M. *Bacchanalia. La répression de 186 av. J.-C. à Rome et en Italie: vestiges, images, traditions* (Rome, 1988)

Scheid, J. 'Graeco ritu: a typically Roman way of honoring the gods', *HSCPh* 97 (1995), 15–31

Empire

Clauss, M. *The Roman Cult of Mithras* (Edinburgh, 2000)

Fishwick, D. *The Imperial Cult in the Latin West. Studies in the Ruler Cult of the Western Provinces of the Roman Empire* 1–2 (Leiden, 1987–1992)

Gordon, R. *Image and Value in the Graeco-Roman world* (Aldershot, 1996)

MacMullen, R. *Paganism in the Roman Empire* (Cambridge, MA, 1981)

Price, S. *Rituals and Power: the Roman Imperial Cult in Asia Minor* (Cambridge, 1984)

Turcan, R. *The Cults of the Roman Empire* (Oxford, 1996)

Weinstock, S. *Divus Julius* (Oxford, 1971)

Le Culte des souverains dans l'empire romain (Entretiens de la Fondation Hardt, 19, Geneva, 1973)

Problems, definitions, ritualism

Durand, J.-L. & J. Scheid ' "Rites" et "religion". Remarques sur certains préjugés des historiens de la religion des Grecs et des Romains', *Archives de Sciences Sociales des Religions* 85 (1994), 23–43

Linder, M. & J. Scheid 'Quand croire c'est faire. Le problème de la croyance dans la Rome ancienne', *Archives de Sciences Sociales des Religions* 81 (1993), 47–62

Scheid, J. 'Polytheism impossible; or, the empty gods: reasons behind a void in the history of Roman religion', in F. Schmidt (ed.), *The Inconceivable Polytheism* (History and Anthropology 3), 303–25 (Paris, 1987)

Calendar

Beard, M. 'A complex of times: no more sheep on Romulus' birthday', *PCPhS* 33 (1987), 1–15

Degrassi, A. *Fasti anni Numani et Iuliani* (*Inscriptiones Italiae* XIII. 2) (Rome, 1963)

Michels, A. K. *The Calendar of the Roman Republic* (Princeton, NJ, 1967)

Rüpke, J. *Kalender und Öffentlichkeit. Die Geschichte der Repräsentation und religiösen Qualifikation von Zeit in Rom* (Berlin & New York, 1995)

Wallace-Hadrill, A. 'Time for Augustus: Ovid, Augustus and the *Fasti*', in M. Whitby et al (eds) *Homo Viator. Classical Essays for John Bramble* (Bristol & Oak Park, Il, 1987), 221–30

Temples, sanctuaries, sacred places

Claridge, A. *Rome* (Oxford, 1998)

Coarelli, F. *Il Foro Romano II. Il Periodo repubblicano e augusteo* (Rome, 1985)

Coarelli, F. *Il Foro Boario dalle origini alla fine della Repubblica* (Rome, 1988)

Coarelli, F. *Guida archeologica di Roma* (Rome, 1995)

Coarelli, F. *Il Campo Marzio* (Rome, 1997)

Gros, P. *Aurea templa. Recherches sur l'architecture religieuse de Rome à l'époque d'Auguste* (Rome, 1976)

Ziolkowski, A. *The Temples of Mid-Republican Rome and their Historical and Topographical Context* (Rome, 1992)

Les Bois sacrées (Actes du colloque international de Naples. Centre Jean-Bérard, 10) (Naples, 1993)

Sacrifice

Freyburger, G. 'La supplication d'action de grâces dans la religion romaine archaique', *Latomus* 36 (1977), 289–98

Freyburger, G. 'La supplication d'action de grâces sous le Haut-Empire', *Aufstieg und Niedergang der römischen Welt* II, 16. 2, 1418–39

Scheid, J. *Romulus et ses frères. Le college des frères arvales, modèle du culte public dans la Rome des empereurs* (Rome, 1990)

Versnel, H. S. (ed.) *Faith, Hope and Worship. Aspects of Religious Mentality in the Ancient World* (Leiden, 1981)

Veyne, P. '*Titulus praelatus*: offrande, solennisation et publicité dans les ex-voto gréco-romains', *Revue Archéologique* 1982–83, 281–300

Veyne, P. 'La nouvelle piété sous l'Empire: s'asseoir auprès des dieux, fréquenter les temples', *RPh* 63 (1989), 175–94

Le sacrifice dans l'Antiquité (Entretiens de la Fondation Hardt, 27, Geneva, 1981)

Divination

Beard, M. 'Cicero and Divination: the formation of a Latin discourse', *JRS* 76 (1986), 33–46

Bloch, R. *La Divination dans l'Antiquité* (Paris, 1984)

Bouché-Leclerq, A. *Histoire de la divination dans l'Antiquité* (Paris, 1892)

Linderski, J. 'Cicero and Roman divination', *Parola del Passato* 37 (1982), 12–38

MacBain, B. *Prodigy and Expiation: a study in religion and politics in Republican Rome* (Brussels, 1982)

Magdelain, A. *Ius imperium auctoritas. Études de droit romain* (Rome, 1990)

North, J. 'Diviners and divination at Rome', in M. Beard & J. North (eds) *Pagan Priests* (London, 1990), 49–71

Scheid, J. 'La parole des dieux. L'originalité du dialogue des Romains avec leurs dieux', *Opus* 6–8 (1987–89), 125–36

Schofield, M. 'Cicero for and against divination', *JRS* 76 (1986), 47–65

Priests and priesthoods

Beard, M. & J. North *Pagan Priests* (London, 1990)

Beard, M. 'The Sexual Status of Vestal Virgins', *JRS* 70 (1980), 12–27

Bouché-Leclerq, A. *Les Pontifes de l'ancienne Rome* (Paris, 1871)

Scheid, J. 'Le flamine de Jupiter, les Vestales et le général triomphant. Variations romaines sur le thème de la figuration des dieux', *Le Temps de la Réflexion* 7 (1986), 213–30

Scheid, J. 'The religious roles of Roman women', in P. Schmitt-Pantel, *A History of Women: from ancient goddesses to Christian saints* (Cambridge, MA, 1992), 377–408

Scheid, J. 'The Priest' in A. Giardina (ed.), *The Romans* (Chicago & London, 1993), 55–84

Gods and Goddesses

Bourgeaud, P. *La Mère des dieux. De Cybèle à la Vierge Marie* (Paris, 1996)

Gagé, J. *L'Apollon romain. Essai sur le culte d'Apollon et le développement du 'ritus Graecus' à Rome des origines à Auguste* (Paris, 1955)

Dubourdieu, A. *Les Origines et le développement du culte des Pénates à Rome* (Rome, 1989)

Le Bonniec, H. *Le Culte de Cérès à Rome, des origines à la fin de la République* (Paris, 1958)

Scheid, J. 'Numa et Jupiter ou les dieux citoyens de Rome', *Archives de Sciences Sociales des Religions* 59 (1985), 41–53

Schilling, R. *La Religion romaine de Vénus* (Paris, 1954)

Tran Tam Tinh, V. *Le Culte d'Isis à Pompei* (Paris, 1964)

Death and Burial

Baldassare, I. 'Sepolture e riti nella necropoli di Isola sacra', *Bollettino di Archeologia* 5 (1990), 49–113

Morris, I. *Death-ritual and social structure in classical antiquity* (Cambridge, 1992)

Scheid, J. 'Contraria facere: renversements et déplacements dans les rites funéraires', *Annali dell'Istituto Orientale di Napoli* 6 (1984), 117–39

Incinération et inhumation dans l'Occident romain aux trois premiers siècles de notre ère (Toulouse, 1987)

INTERPRETATIONS

Philosophy

Griffin, M. & J. Barnes, *Philosophia Togata: essays on philosophy and Roman society* (Oxford, 1989)

Long, A. A. & D. Sedley, *The Hellenistic Philosophers* (Cambridge, 1987)

Myth

In addition to the work of G. Dumézil:

Bremmer, J. & N. Horsfall (eds), *Roman Myth and Mythography* (London, 1987)

Burkert, W. *Ancient Mystery Cults* (Cambridge, MA, 1987)

Detienne, M. *The Creation of Mythology* (Chicago, 1986)

Graf, F. (ed.), *Mythos in mythenloser Gesellschaft. Das Paradigma Roms* (Colloquium Rauricum 3, Stuttgart & Leipzig, 1993)

Veyne, P. *Did the Greeks believe in their Myths* (Chicago, 1988)

Images

Ryberg, I. Scott, *Rites of the State Religion in Roman Art* (Memoirs of the American Academy at Rome, Rome, 1955)

Torelli, M. *Typology and Structure of Roman Historical Reliefs* (Ann Arbor, 1982)

Other religions

Beard, M. 'The Roman and the foreign: the cult of the 'Great Mother' in imperial Rome', in N. Thomas & C. Humphrey (eds), *Shamanism, History and the State* (Ann Arbor, 1994), 164–90

Brashear, W. M. *A Mithraic Catechism from Egypt <P. Berol. 21196>* (Vienna, 1992)

Lane-Fox, R. *Pagans and Christians in the Mediterranean World from the Second Century AD to the Conversion of Constantine* (Harmondsworth & New York, 1986)

North, J. 'Religious Toleration in Republican Rome', *PCPhS* 25 (1979), 85–103

Index